MW00779095

My Memory is Eroding

The 10 Reasons Why I Decided to Start Glory Day™ Brain Booster

Richard P. Johnson, PhD

"When your brain works better... your life does too"

ISBN 978-0-9903384-4-4

10 9 8 7 6 5 4 3 2 1

First Edition

Printed in the United States of America

In Gratitude

I want to personally thank Susan Gibson; her inspiration, professional creativity, and human compassion has given hope to all of us who suffer from memory slippage.

1. *I thank you Susan for digging deeply into your professional expertise to formulate Glory Day Brain Booster; to put together just the right ingredients, in exactly right proportions to help us all.*

2. *I also thank you for your unselfish help to me identifying the many professional journal articles that report the research on the nine ingredients in Glory Day Brain Booster. Your assistance, which has measurably up-stepped this book is deeply appreciated.*

So… from me and from all those of us who have, and will benefit from your unselfish work…

Thank you Susan!

Susan Gibson, the formulator of Glory Day Brain Booster would like you to have the valuable "Brain Health Habits Assessment" absolutely free. I have used it myself (and with others) to excellent effect. It's the easiest and quickest way to assess your brain health habits. Just log onto Vivolor.com and click on Brain Health Habits Assessment.

Please know that I have no monetary interest in Glory Day Brain Booster, or its producer, Vivolor Therapeutics. I wrote this book simply because I use, trust and have benefited from Glory Day Brain Booster, and wanted other people to know about it.

Richard P. Johnson, PhD.

Foreword

Why I wrote this book…

I'm not one to dive into something new without due diligence; and starting Glory Day Brain Booster was, for me a big decision indeed that required some thoughtful investigation.

I can beat myself up for making mistakes. My sometimes low self-esteem dictates that I investigate new endeavors thoroughly; I can really put myself down hard if I don't first investigate. I'm not skeptical, but I am thoughtfully thorough.

Most of my writing (see Appendices 3, 4 and 5) involves lots of investigation before I write even one word. I'm a firm believer in the maxim my father taught me, *"Measure twice… cut once!"* I've used this advice over-and-over across my lifespan, and certainly here in my intentional decision about Glory Day Brain Booster.

So this book is the result of my due-diligence. In these pages I describe (as best I can) the 10 reasons I decided to start taking Glory Day Brain Booster. I also report the fruits of my investigation into the nine ingredients in the formulary of Glory Day Brain Booster. The research findings I uncovered in my investigations truly convinced me that Glory Day Brain Booster was indeed what I needed.

It's my sincere hope that you will find this book informative and interesting. I also want you to know that I wrote this book on my own volition, based solely because I believe in the product. I neither have received, nor will receive any monetary compensation from the company that owns and distributes Glory Day Brain Booster, nor from anyone else.

Richard P. Johnson, PhD

PS: I wrote another book titled, "My Memory Is Awakening: My First 30 Days Taking Glory Day Brain Booster," that's also available. The book is my introspective journal of the positive changes I noticed in my body, mind and spirit during my first month taking Glory Day.

Visit amazon.com/author/richardpjohnson to find that book as well as several other titles I've written about mental, emotional, and spiritual well-being.

Contents

Introduction

My Brain

My brain is the most important organ I possess. As Dr. Daniel G. Amen, MD writes,

"Brain health is central to all health in life. When your brain works right, you are happier, healthier, wealthier, and more successful in everything you do. When your brain is troubled, for whatever reason, you are likely to be sadder, sicker, poorer, and less successful." (1)

My brain is the seat, and the operating system of my personality. All six functions of my personality are formulated, structured and delivered by my brain: all I 1) believe, 2) perceive, 3) think, 4) feel, 5) decide, and every 6) action is all conceived of, and governed by my brain (see Appendix One). If my brain begins to slip, so does my life. As my brain goes, so goes my life. If I wish to live my life fully, happily, and optimally; I need a healthy brain.

I'm the owner and caretaker of my brain.

I literally shudder when I stop to think if the horrible consequences to my life if my brain begins shutting-down. My personality unravels: my inner life compass (my internal "data operating system") evaporates; my capacity for taking in new data of any kind gradually darkens; my ability to think and live a meaningful life melts into nothingness; I lose touch with my emotions; I can no longer make decisions; and my capacity for intentional action fades into blankness. I do remember the fear I experienced when I was in the US Army many years ago, but that fear pales when I think of the darkness of dementia.

As my brain goes, so goes my life.

I need to do all that I can to care for my brain, feed it correctly, give it proper rest, and most of all make sure it has the best nutrients. I want and need to treat my brain as the precious instrument of my body, and director of my life that it is. This is no small responsibility... I'm the owner and caretaker of my brain. And that is why I'm so glad I found Glory Day™ Brain Booster!

Here are the reasons I decided to start taking Glory Day Brain Booster:

1. To enhance my memory

2. To help with my fear of dementia

3. To "ward-off" my tendency toward depression

4. To stabilize my heart disease

5. To contain my cancer

6. To accelerate my healing

7. To age well

8. To energize my positive mental attitude and overall well-being

9. To smile more freely and frequently

10. To develop new resilience

Please note that Glory Day™ Brain Booster is a dietary supplement. It has not been evaluated in clinical trials. Glory Day Brain Booster is not intended to diagnose, treat, cure or prevent any disease.

Chapter One

Reason 1: To Enhance My Memory

I suffer from what I call "selective memory". This is far-and-away the number one reason why I decided to start Glory Day. I can effortlessly focus on and remember dates, times, prices, and my counseling patients' history. I can literally remember the diagnosis, my treatment, their own history, family dynamics, indeed all their "pertinent details", but if you ask me their name, I sometimes draw a blank. The same is true for books and movies - I remember the plot, the setting, the conversations, etc., but don't ask me the characters names, or the title of the book or movie.

I've always had this problem; the psychiatric name for this is "memory-slippage" is <u>anomia</u>, the inability to remember names. But over the past several years my "secret malady" has worsened; it has penetrated deeper into my life and shown-up in more noticeable ways.

I do a fair amount of public speaking: give classes, seminars, workshops and retreats. I've always enjoyed this part of my work/ministry. I do remember the first time I was embarrassed when I couldn't "pull-up" the name of a famous psychologist author. Fear shot through me when I stopped dumbfounded in the middle of a sentence, unable to speak.

I've given talks to groups as large as 500+; I used to say *"the bigger the better."* But my enthusiasm waned, replaced by a waxing apprehension that I would be "caught" flat-footed in a memory slippage that muted me mid-sentence, creating a pause that seemed an eternity.

Such lapses became more noticeable to me and probably my students/audiences as well. My concern for my memory slips escalated; and triggered a growing apprehension that broke into fear. I started feeling anxious. The pangs of stage fright only worsened my memory problem.

Something had to change before my apprehension morphed into an emotional freeze that would stop me from speaking publicly altogether. I needed my memory lapses to stop, at least enough so my anxiety wouldn't take over.

I also began noticing that my memory slippage started popping up in another very disturbing way. While "hanging-out" with even my closest friends, I would at times, struggle to find the "right" word. I'm an author, and am necessarily a "word-smith." I guess I want to find the word that best describes what I'm trying to communicate. I like precise descriptions; I guess I take some delight (perhaps pride) in using precise language. I consider it something of a failure if/when I use three or four words to say what could have been said, perhaps even more precisely, with only one.

I became a bit alarmed as I found myself not infrequently stopped mid-sentence unable to find that most descriptive word. I felt confounded as my pauses in speech became longer and more frequent. I felt embarrassed, almost ashamed that I was somehow verbally "sinning" by omission.

I became very self-conscious; words weren't flowing as they always had. I was stumbling through my words and my speech. I knew there was a great word that would absolutely make my thoughts crystal clear, but my brain wouldn't let me grab it! Without conscious intention, I started holding back from conversation. I was losing my self-confidence!

I wouldn't say that I became non-communicative, but I certainly was not contributing to the conversation like I formerly did. I was beginning to feel a bit out-of-step, a bit unsure that I could complete the sentence when I started it. Consequently, I felt the emotional sting of being on the fringe of the group; a fear that I was becoming just a bit distant from the natural and comfortable social connection I formerly enjoyed.

I was even becoming somewhat apprehensive to enter into social discourse... unsure, a bit unstable, and certainly sad about this ominously advancing vacancy in social "performance." An advancing grip of social anxiety began squeezing my formerly comfortable social group familiarity.

That's when I discovered Glory Day. I was more than surprised to discover that all nine ingredients of Glory Day have scientific publications describing their beneficial effects on memory.

1. Pine Bark Extract: The following studies have shown that pine bark extract boosts brain function, improves memory, response speed, sustained attention, executive function and mental clarity. (2,3,4,5,6)

2. Lion's Mane Mushroom: The referenced publications outline lion's manes improvements in the functioning of the hippocampus (a major structure of the limbic system of the brain). Lion's Mane has also been shown to enhance cognitive function and improve memory. (7,8,9,10)

3. Bacopa Monnieri: Multiple references describe studies where bacopa improved communication between neurons (the communication structures of the brain), prevented memory loss, improved learning and improved information processing speed. (11,12,13, 14,15,16,17,18)

4. L-Theanine: Data are cited where L-theanine improved mental performance, alertness and attention as well as reduced memory loss. (19,20,21,22,23,24,25,26,27)

5. Resveratrol: Resveratrol has been broadly researched as a nootropic (memory enhancer). These scientific papers show it to be a substance that protected against cognitive impairment, improved psychomotor speed and long-term memory, and enhanced brain health. (28,29,30,31,32,33,34,35,36)

6. Tamarix: Tamarix has been published as a potent anti-oxidant that inhibits cognitive impairment. (37,38,39,40,41,42)

7. DHA: DHA is an omega-3 fatty acid shown to promote overall brain health by fighting age-related mental decline in these references. It also improved visual

memory, short-term memory, working memory, vocabulary, attention and speed. (43,44,45,46,47)

8. Curcumin: Studies of curcumin show that it enhances cognition, attention, alertness, psychomotor speed and memory. (48,49,50,51,52,53)

9. Ginkgo Biloba: Publications describe gingko's effects as having improved coordination, memory, attention, and cognition. (54,55,56,57,58)

Chapter Two

Reason 2: To Help with my Fear of Dementia

My paternal grandmother was plagued by Alzheimer's Disease (AD). Slowly but surely, and unceasingly she descended into the depths of unknowing. As long as I can remember, I picture her sitting... just sitting in her chair with a vacant face and a seemingly blank mind. Gramma was a rather docile patient; thankfully she was not irritated, combative, delusional, or critical... she just "wasn't there." I never knew her any other way.

My Aunt Mary devoted her life to Gramma. Aunt Mary never married; her life was taken in service to Gramma. In a very real way, I witnessed both Gramma's life and Aunt Mary's life fade into the darkness of AD.

In the books, and lectures, and study of the aging process, I came face-to-face with the ravages of AD and the other dementias. In the process, I gained new understanding and appreciation for the horrors of AD and the life contorting rigors of caregivers – those who literally give their lives in unheralded service to loved ones, or patients with AD.

It was no coincidence that my first published book was devoted to helping caregivers. I dedicated the book titled "Because I Care... Inspiration for Caregivers" to my Aunt Mary (available on Amazon at amzn.to/2xecgrw).

I became somewhat consumed with helping caregivers. In my position as Director of Behavioral Medicine in a large teaching hospital, I was pushed (actually I think divinely inspired) to start caregiver support groups, write a caregiver's monthly newsletter, and give dozens of talks on caregiving in the city, region, and eventually all around the country.

I hold caregivers of any type in the highest esteem. Here's what I said in the preface of one of my books on caregiving...

I have so much empathy for caregivers — these armies of people pressed into service in the sometimes messy and always taxing trenches of caregiving with little or no warning and even less assistance. They had no idea that they were forfeiting so much at that very moment, that their lives would never be the same again, nor that they would be forced to not only confront illness, but also forced to face themselves in ways both challenging and demanding they've not dreamed of before. This book is dedicated to all those who give care to persons with illness or other issues. These devoted folks, regardless of where and how they serve, are truly the unsung soldiers and heroes of the illness wars. (1)

My experience and memory of my grandmother and Aunt Mary pushed me on in my mission of studying gerontology, writing my observations and thoughts about aging, and serving in the field my entire professional life. All along, and perhaps deep in my subconscious, there hides an ever-present fear that I too might fall to the same fate as my grandmother, and so push my wife into my Aunt Mary's fate as well.

Fear of dementia, and especially Alzheimer's Disease, is the second big reason I wholeheartedly welcomed Glory Day into my life. I need to do whatever I can to take care of my brain and prevent memory loss from taking hold of me, and my wife. My investigation into Glory Day Brain Booster tells me Glory Day can improve my memory today, but as importantly, Glory Day seems potent to calm the fires of inflammation and oxidation that fuel the pathology that may lead to more memory loss. Glory Day appears to buffer the brain by providing valuable nutrients that reinvigorate the brain to possibly forestall the onset of dementia. I believe that Glory Day can keep my brain as healthy as possible.

I've investigated all nine of the nutrient "ingredients" of Glory Day; I've done my homework on Glory Day. What I found impressed me greatly: every one of the nutrients in Glory Day has statistical data evidence that it does have a positive effect on memory. Many of the nutrients may actually help regenerate neurons which not only degenerate over time, but because of the normal aging process, my body (and yours) gradually loses its ability to regenerate my neuronal structures in my brain.

1. Lion's Mane Mushroom: Lion's man contains over 70 potent bioactive compounds, vitamins and minerals (including hericenones and erinacines) described in the literature as anti-aging and neuro-protective. Studies have shown that it helps repair nerves, induces nerve growth and increases nerve myelin sheath formation to help preserve normal brain health (2,3,4,5,6)

2. Bacopa monnieri: There are publications about bacopa protecting nerves, preventing cognitive deficits and increasing blood flow in the brain (7,8,9,10,11,12,13):

3. Tamarix: Tamarix contains flavonoids that have been shown to protect cells and stop cell death (14,15,16)

4. DHA (Omega-3 fish oil): DHA is the most important natural fat in your brain. Low levels of DHA have been associated with Alzheimer's disease. High levels of DHA have been associated with reduced loss of neurons, reduced brain shrinkage, and improved neurotransmission. Studies show that increasing levels of DHA improved cognition. In 1 study, those with the highest DHA levels showed a 65% reduced risk of all-cause dementia and a 60-72% reduced risk of Alzheimer's disease (17,18,19,20,21)

5. Curcumin: These references refer to curcumin preventing neurodegeneration, enhancing neuron function, promoting neurogenesis and neural plasticity, and beneficially influencing neurotransmitters. (22,23,24,25,26)

6. Ginkgo Biloba: These studies who gingko as neuroprotective and describe improvements in cognitive function in Alzheimer's disease and mild cognitive impairment (27,28,29,30)

7. Resveratrol: A number of published articles expound on resveratrol as neuroprotective, can delay age-related cognitive decline, supports healthy expression

of genes associated with slowing aging, improves neuroplasticity and can protect against Alzheimer's disease (31,32,33,34,35,36,37,38)

8. L-Theanine: Papers describe L-theanine as neuroprotective, increases some neurotransmitters, may promote restorative sleep and reduces toxins (39,40,41,42,43,44,45,46)

9. Pine bark extract: This study shows pine bark as enhancing synaptic plasticity (47)

Chapter Three

Reason 3: To "Ward Off" my Tendency toward Depression

I've never been formally diagnosed with depression, nor have I ever taken anti-depressant medication. Yet, I have many times experienced sadness, self-blame, irritability/anger, fear, emotional pain, and guilt (and more), all indicators of depression. One of my books, "Healing and Depression: Finding Peace in the Midst of Transition, Turmoil, or Illness" (available on Amazon at amzn.to/34tQkEG) offers a comprehensive look at how to address depression.

Perhaps I'm so sensitive to depression because I've seen and treated so many patients with depression. I've been with them through their tears, their inner torment, their self-blaming (loathing), their dark nights of the soul, their sense of unworthiness, and all the rest. I felt/feel all of this keenly, and come to identify with the emotional jumble of feelings so pressing on them, that I no doubt have taken depressive feelings into my own heart and soul.

I've been blessed (perhaps cursed) with an exceptional sensitivity, and a keen empathy that together allow me to identify, share, and suffer with my struggling patients to such a degree that I have no doubt that my emotions sometimes mesh with theirs. Call this a professional hazard or an implicit predisposition to a DNA driven susceptibility to depression, or some combination, one igniting the other, that serves to press me into periods of persecution which push me to seek inner islands of peace, that could confront the terrible push of inner pressures I experience.

All this emotional press motivated me to write books on mental wellness, depression, inner wisdom, low self-esteem, and more (see Appendix 3). When I look at the more than 40 books I've written, I realize that in some part I wrote them for me. I also believe that because I felt the fangs of depression, I was well prepared to help those people who came to me for help, and to write about depression in a heartfelt, convincing and genuine way. So, in some paradoxical way my struggles with depression helped me to help others gain adequate inspiration and inner light to climb out of their own dark wells of depression.

My depressive low points rob me of my usual zest. They leave me lifeless and sad, angry and irritable, stressed and easily overwhelmed. Depression twists my soul leaving me destabilized, un-centered, and unfocused, and consequently more vulnerable to slipping into my shadows and compulsions. Depression contorts my personality leaving me less able to resist any noxious emotional, psychological, and spiritual forces that may accompany me.

Depression is a reaction to what's been called "dissonance" in my personality. Dissonance is another name for internal tension, emotional clutter, discontent, and dissension, all mixed up with the spiritual "gunpowder" of fear. In other words, depression signals an undeclared inner war against my personality.

My depressive bouts squeeze virtue from my soul, pushing me into a shadowland. These battles overthrow me and confuse me; they can make me feel like I'm living in a state of emotional trench warfare where I not only feel under attack, but I feel helpless to do anything about it.

- When I'm feeling down, my brain isn't working correctly.
- My beliefs lack the hope-power required for personal direction.
- My perceptions seem complex and confused.
- My thoughts lack any wisdom.
- My feelings are obtuse and infecting rather than motivational.
- My decisions are conflicted at best, and more likely simply frozen.
- My behaviors are stiff, stilted, repressed, and stifled, lacking any vitality, zest or inspiration. (1)

I cannot imagine that I will ever return to a peaceful state from this darkness.

When I saw the mental health benefits of the ingredients Susan has brought together and assayed in exactly the right proportions, there was no doubt that Glory Day Brain Booster was for me.

1. Curcumin: The studies referenced show that curcumin reduces physical and mental fatigue, increases

calmness, enhances contentedness, improves sustained attention and improves resilience in response to stress. Curcumin appears to have an anti-fatigue effect. A meta-analysis of 6 randomized controlled human clinical trials showed evidence of efficacy and safety of curcumin in treatment of major depressive disorder with significantly reduced depression symptoms. (2,3,4)

2. Bacopa monnieri: Randomized, double-blind, placebo-controlled trials have shown that bacopa reduced anxiety and depression. (5,6,7)

3. Lion's Mane mushroom: The references highlight lion's mane for improving anxiety, fighting fatigue, and data suggest a beneficial role in depression. (8,9,10)

4. Pine bark: These articles show pine bark improves mood, fatigue, sleeping and sustained attention and reduces irritability (11,12,13,14)

5. L-Theanine: L-theanine has been shown to relax the mind, increase attention and alertness, reduce stress and anxiety and improve sleep quality. An open label study in patients with major depressive disorder showed statistically significant improvement in depression (15,16,17,18,19,20,21,22)

6. Gingko biloba: A human clinical study in elderly patients with depression showed that gingko biloba reduced depression and anxiety. Time to onset of

efficacy was faster with Gingko combined with anti-depressants than with anti-depressants alone (23)

7. Resveratrol: 22 animal studies suggest that resveratrol may be an effective treatment for depression. (24,25,26,27)

Please note that the FDA has not reviewed these data. Glory Day Brain Booster is not indicated for the treatment of depression. Glory Day is a dietary supplement and is not intended to diagnose or treat disease.

Chapter Four

Reason 4: To Stabilize my Heart Disease

My family, especially the males in my lineage have all died of heart disease – my paternal grandfather died at his office desk as age 51; my father died at 57; his three brothers died suddenly of heart attack ages, 48, 60, and 74, my mother at 71; my younger brother at 47, my older brother (a physician who took excellent care if his body, mind and spirit) at 74. Our middle son had a heart stint inserted at age 41! Me, I had a very startling 7-way cardiac arterial bypass at age 54. Yes, my history is clear. And I am not alone, since heart disease is still the #1 cause of death in the western world and now globally.

I was flummoxed when I experienced my first "heart incident" that led to my cardiac bypass surgery. I assumed that heart disease would shorten my life, that it would take time away from me. I didn't realize that I worshipped the "god" of longevity. I thought that the longer I lived, the more birthdays I celebrated, then all-the-better for me.

Once I dropped this veil of confusion and anger, I could better see that I had been living in the future; for me today was only valuable for what it could produce for tomorrow. Consequently, I could never truly live in the present, because I "lived" in tomorrow." Heart disease has shown me the value of today quite apart from the future. I'm not promised a future. I'm only given today. Indeed, I'm only given "now." This "now" is only valuable to the degree that I choose to make it valuable.

My heart disease teaches me that the "now" is much more than a measure of time. Today, right now, is a heartbeat of the eternal that makes it a sacred instant. I can embrace my "now" as an inspirational moment to the degree that I invest it with the vitality of my spiritual strengths. When I connect this "now" with the eternal presence in me, whatever the moment is, I realize just how packed with the power of Presence this "now" is for me.

Today I strive to live in the holy present ... the "now." (1)

I wish to make today my finest hour, and I think my heart disease, when seen in a wider, more profound perspective might help me in this goal.

Before my heart attack I was so driven by achievement, by producing "things," to the degree that I only saw "my finest hours" as those times of greatest personal production. Any year that passed without generating a new book was at least uninspiring if not wasteful to me. I still "produce" books, but I no longer need to for myself. My finest hours are now those spent in the presence of my inner strengths.

When a final accounting of my life is taken, what moments will stand-out as my finest hours? My heart disease has given me a new answer to this question. My time with heart disease with its struggles, its doubts, fears, pain, and expense... all of its demands will, I believe, be counted as at least one of my finest hours indeed.

Today I live as this "now" is my finest hour.

I try diligently to fold into my life every lifestyle change I can – diet, exercise, stress reduction, etc., etc., to strengthen my heart, to lighten my load, to arrange my environment, to live in gratitude, peace, and simplicity, and to intentionally follow the purpose of soul that I've been given. I do all this to protect my heart and fortify my life with the tools of heaven.

As I ponder all this body, mind and spirit work, I can see a place for Glory Day Brain Booster in the mix. I'm looking for something that can somehow help my body, my mind, and my spirit... something that can serve as a daily cohesive force pulling all parts of me together. I know all this may sound a bit "out there" but I'll tell you something I don't believe I've ever exposed.

Every morning as I take my prescription pills I think of each pill and capsule as gifts: gifts of human intelligence, gifts of the earth, and gifts of the cosmos. I imagine these gifts traveling through my body healing, and soothing me. I imagine them as lights illuminating and filling any deficiencies, smoothing any "rough spots", and generally bringing all my inner tissues, organs, and structures to health.

This is what I mean by a cohesive force, and I decided on Glory Day Brain Booster because after investigating its ingredients I was impressed to find several that have clear benefits for my heart. Heart disease is also a risk factor for memory loss and dementia (2,3,4). The heart disease itself revs up the pathology that leads to memory loss (3,6,7). So, it is important to address heart disease both for my heart and for my brain.

1. DHA: Studies show DHA lowers triglycerides (cholesterol) in the blood, reduces blood pressure, lowers risk of thrombosis (stroke) and prevents cardiac arrhythmias. Epidemiological studies have shown reductions over 50% in sudden death from myocardial infarction (heart attack) with consuming DHA from fish. DHA also has shown a positive effect on hypertension, adult-onset diabetes, and myocardial infarction (heart attacks) (8,9,10,11,12)

2. Resveratrol: References cited show resveratrol promotes cardiovascular health, protects the heart and circulatory system, lowers cholesterol and protects against blood clots which can cause heart attacks and stroke. It also crosses the blood-brain barrier and increases brain blood flow. Resveratrol has been shown to increase endothelial function, cardiac remodeling, myocardial energetics, vascular function and reduce cardiac fibrosis. Some evidence implies potential benefits in heart failure (13,14,15,16)

3. Gingko biloba: These studies demonstrate reduced blood lipids, reduced blood sugar, improved glucose regulation, reduced heart disease, improved blood circulation, and reduced cardiovascular reactivity to

cognitive tasks. There is some evidence gingko might attenuate atherosclerosis (17,18,19)

4. Lion's mane mushroom: the publication including here show lion's mane reduces hypertension, is cardio-protective, lowers blood cholesterol, improves lipids, and reduces blood glucose (20,21,22,23)

5. Curcumin: Articles show curcumin improves blood lipids and cholesterol (24)

6. L-theanine: L-theanine has reduced blood cholesterol (25)

Chapter Five

Reason 5: To Contain my Cancer

At age 24 I found myself a soldier in the U.S. Army in the former Republic of Viet Nam. While there, I was exposed to the chemical defoliant we all called "Agent Orange." Agent Orange was everywhere! Only later was Agent Orange discovered to be a potent carcinogen. And yes, at age 61, I was diagnosed with cancer.

What's the treatment? Well, my doctors wanted to remove my prostate ASAP. Two of my brothers are physicians (the elder has since died), and both argued strenuously that I should not go that route. They both recommended a plan now called "active surveillance." This basically means that I team-up with my primary care physician; together we watch my prostate as closely as possible. You can visit https://spiritualstrengths.org/pages/cancer-survivor to learn more about a series of books I wrote about cancer, including a free ebook titled, "From Cancer Survivor to New Life Thriver."

I have my PSA test done every six months; any wide changes would require an immediate prostate biopsy to see if the cancer had spread. So far there has been no need for biopsy. So, I live on the edge; I do wonder about a cancer "flare-up." Yet, I have a life to live, I have a desire to thrive, and this is where Glory Day Brain Booster comes in.

Please note that I am in no way recommending active surveillance to all men diagnosed with prostate cancer. There are different kinds of cancer, some much more aggressive than others.

I'm now considered a cancer survivor. A survivor is one who continues to live, or simply exists. I don't want to simply exist; no, I want to thrive even with my cancer. A thriver is one who continues to grow with vigor and flourish. So why do so many cancer survivors remain stuck in a continuous survival mentality, unable to break free into thriver-mode?

One of the big problems for cancer survivors is the ever-present fear that "demon cancer" might come back. This toxic thought follows cancers survivors like an ominous shadow. Sometimes the thought sits in the corner like a quiet kitten; other times it sits on your chest like a guerilla.

Certainly, I'm glad I am a survivor, but I don't want to be stuck in survivorship. I know I'm lucky to be a survivor, and I am grateful for it. I thank God; I even ask, "Why me Lord, how did I get so lucky when so many others didn't?" But that's a question I can't answer. All I know is that I'm still here; I'm still "kicking." But then I ask, "Is this all there is – survival?" I ask, "Survival for what?" There must be a purpose here; there must be a plan, and somehow, I'm supposed to participate in it. I can't simply be a passive observer of this grand gift of survivorship – I need to embrace it, not simply accept it.

That's when it hit me that I needed to take the next step beyond survivorship and become a thriver. My true inner self was pushing me to stick my head above the foxhole of survivorship and see what's 'out there.' What I discovered is 'out there' is a whole new world, a world I call thriver-mode; and I decided that Glory Day Brain Booster could be a big part of my thriver-mode.

I'm an author; I'd already written 20 books on various spiritual topics when cancer visited me. I'm also a professional, board certified counselor, with a private practice, and had worked for 15 years teaching medical interns and residents the 'art of medicine' so they could relate better with their patients. I was no stranger to the medical community and to the reality of cancer when it first 'tapped me on my shoulder.'

Like the "Hound of Heaven" in Francis Thompson's famous poem by the same title, the Holy Spirit pursued me. The Spirit grabbed my head and heart and hand, sat me down and didn't let go until I wrote what I needed to do to start on my own road to thriver-mode. You can visit https://spiritualstrengths.org/pages/cancer-survivor to learn more about a series of books I wrote about cancer, including a free ebook titled, "From Cancer Survivor to New Life Thriver."

When I was first diagnosed with cancer, I threw myself into the "land of cancer" by reading, learning, questioning, investigating, etc., etc., etc., about cancer. Ultimately, I found myself consumed in and by my cancer. Cancer had not only invaded my body, but it had also overtaken my mind. I needed a break.

I then discovered the psychology of leisure and its primary and paradoxical tenet, *"I must regularly vacate my routines in order to remain focused upon them."* What a revelation! My routines now all revolved around cancer, so it was cancer that I needed to "regularly vacate." But how could I achieve this... and by what means? I needed to have fun. (2)

Fun removes me from my routines; it gives me a vacation from cancer. I struggle with this because, while I enjoy fun and vacations, I've always felt a bit guilty about them because... well... I can't get anything done!

I started "working" on leisure, but quickly realized the contradiction here. I now try to "flow" with the moment, finding my leisure, my fun, in contemplation, discussion, social interaction, and spectator appreciation (I like to watch people). Today I find fun.

To remedy my inner angst, I re-activated my own personal healing blueprint – I started writing books to inspire cancer patients and survivors. At last count I've written eight books on cancer. The process of writing wrung all the anger out of me and replaced it with a Spirit-given hope, patience, resilience, and peace. I am so grateful for this inner transformation.

During my investigation of Glory Day Brain Booster, I was thrilled to discover that some of the ingredients of Glory Day have been researched and found to have positive benefits for persons with cancer. This information not only gave me positive pause, but more importantly provided an inner confidence and even a bit of solace that I was doing all I could to hold back the demon of cancer. I am not recommending that anyone skip any cancer treatments they've been advised to take. And this is not medical advice.

But many of the ingredients in Glory Day Brain Booster have been shown to have beneficial results in various types of cancer.

1. Curcumin: In the following references, curcumin has shown many anti-cancer activities including inhibiting cell proliferation (multiplying of cancer cells), inhibiting transcription factors that impact genes, modulating cell-signaling pathways, and affecting growth factor receptors and cell adhesion molecules that are involved in the growth, blood flow and spreading of the cancer. Curcumin demonstrated in vivo suppression of growth of head and neck cancers. Intravenous curcumin inhibited oral cancer growth. Cancer growth suppression increased when curcumin was taken in combination with other anti-cancer drugs compared to either agent alone. Curcumin may also enhance cancer radiation therapy. Studies showed that curcumin plus radiation had better suppression of cancer growth than either curcumin or radiation alone. Clinical trials are ongoing or completed for various cancers, including breast, pancreatic and colorectal cancers, and multiple myeloma (3,4,5,6,7,8,9,10,11)

2. Resveratrol: Studies of resveratrol showed promising effects in inhibiting cell proliferation, inducing cell death and hindering cancer progression in several cancer models. It may show promise in sensitizing cancer cells to chemotherapy and radiation. Results in animals and humans vary depending on dose, cancer type and many other factors, so more work is

needed to understand potential applications. (12.13.14)

3. DHA: Women with high levels of DHA have reduced risk of breast cancer. Studies of DHA as a preventative for breast cancer are underway. DHA may help alleviate some side effects of chemotherapy. DHA may reduce risk of prostate cancer and may be helpful in head and neck cancer. (15,16,17,18,19)

4. Tamarisk ingredient quercetin: Anti-cancer properties of quercetin have been seen in the literature and include inhibiting cell signaling, enhancing cell death, hindering cell multiplication, anti-oxidant effects and suppressing growth. It may also have synergy with chemotherapy or radiation treatments (20,21,22)

Chapter Six

Reason 6: To Accelerate my Healing

Over three years ago I got my annual flu shot; ten days later I was a virtual quadriplegic — absolutely unable to move my hands, arms, feet and legs. I was bed-bound. On the third day in the ER I was diagnosed with Guillain-Barre Syndrome — a very rare disorder that causes your own immune system to attack the sheathing around your nerves called myelin. When the myelin sheathing is damaged no impulses can get through to your muscles — they are rendered inoperable. Consequently, my muscles began to atrophy due to the disease, rendering me paralyzed of hands, arms, feet and legs.

After six weeks of therapy, I learned to use a power chair. I moved the 500+ pound behemoth forward by blowing into a tube attached to the steering mechanism and positioned right at my lips. I went backward by sucking in on the tube. With a halo mechanism around my head, I could turn right by tapping twice on the right side of the halo with my head; left doing the same on the left side of the halo. Such was my mobility. I graduated to a regular wheelchair six months later, a walker a year after that, and now to a cane.

During this recuperation I had 26 intravenous drug infusions, three surgeries on my hands, and constant physical and occupational therapy. While I'm much, much better, I'm certainly not "all better" and perhaps never will be.

As I look back on those early days in therapy one thing is striking to me. Maybe I shouldn't be surprised because I worked in the medical community for 15 years. At no time during this journey was I ever advised about nutrition, or any dietary supplement or nutraceutical that might help me.

Guillain-Barre is entirely a neurological disorder. Glory Day Brain Booster's ingredients have been studied for their benefits in neurological regeneration. Glory Day provides nutrients that create a favorable environment for neurons to flourish and grow. This is exactly what I needed. Pharmaceuticals (prescription drugs) that are approved for the treatment of Alzheimer's disease do not impact the underlying disease or delay progression of dementia.

Is the medical community ignorant of the inherent value of nutraceuticals, or are they somehow prejudiced against them? For most physicians it is both! When I recently informed my cardiologist I was taking Glory Day, his "kneejerk" reaction was to "inform" (lecture) me that nutraceuticals do not go through the same rigor as FDA approved pharmaceuticals. This "advice" wasn't helpful for me at all.

No, I'm not thinking of changing cardiologists; I believe he is a good medical doctor, and I trust his medical advice. I simply can't rely on him for counsel about potential options for me that are outside his purview. Such is the state of medicine today... it's wonderful, and even "miraculous" in what it can achieve. But medicine like everything on this earth has its limits. And physicians are trained to diagnose and treat disease. They are not trained in nutrition, disease prevention or health optimization.

Now, every morning as I take me Glory Day Brain Booster, I imagine my entire nervous system – brain, heart, prostate, arms, legs and everything in between and around is receiving activating and regenerating nutrients. I'm compliant with what the medical community tells me, and I'm also intentional about using properly, intelligently and thoughtfully prepared additional healing agents such as Glory Day Brain Booster as well.

There is quite a bit of evidence that Glory Day ingredients are neuro-protective, enhance nerve and neuron growth and survival, and enhance nerve signal conduction.

1. Bacopa: Some studies of bacopa show it protects nerves and promotes nerve and neuron survival (1,2,3,4,5,6)

2. Curcumin: Curcumin has been seen to prevent neurodegeneration, enhance neuron function, promote growth of new neurons (neurogenesis and neural plasticity), increase neuron signaling, and beneficially influence neurotransmitters (7,8,9,10,11)

3. DHA: DHA is a structural component of the membranes of neurons and nerves. DHA is essential to healthy brain development and function throughout life. DHA is important for neuron growth,

differentiation, and signaling. Studies show that loss of DHA from the nerve cell membrane leads to dysfunction. DHA is neuroprotective, supports brain cell survival and repair, inhibits neuron cell death and helps signaling. (12, 13,14,15)

4. Pine bark: Pine bark has been reported to have anti-oxidant properties that help maintain normal cellular function attenuating oxidative reaction and cell death. In vitro studies showed it increased gene expression and helped protect cells from damage. Pine bark may protect against some toxicities from chemotherapeutic agents (16,17,18,19,20,21,22)

5. Lion's mane mushroom: There is evidence of lion's mane inducing nerve growth, repairing nerves, and increasing myelin sheath formation on nerves (23,24,25,26)

6. L-theanine: L-theanine appears to promote proliferation of neurons and neuronal commitment and enhance signaling pathways. Literature implies L-theanine may promote nerve regeneration through its anti-oxidant and inti-inflammatory effects (27,28)

7. Tamarisk: Articles on tamarisk show it potentially protects cells, stops cell death and has potent anti-oxidant effects. An ingredient in Tamarisk called Quercetin is believed to be one of the most powerful natural neuroprotective agents. It has been shown in models to protect against damage from neurotoxic chemicals, neuronal injury and neurodegenerative diseases. In addition to a possible direct antioxidant

effect, quercetin may also act by stimulating cellular defenses against oxidative stress, inducing antioxidant/anti-inflammatory enzymes and inducing autophagy (29,30,31,32,33,34)

8. Resveratrol: Some studies of resveratrol show it improves neuroplasticity and induces autophagy (35,36,37)

Chapter Seven

Reason 7: To Age Well

I'm very aware that my body and mind are both aging. I see the effects of aging literally from my head to my toes. My graduate gerontology certification program thoroughly informed me about how the "normal" aging process slowly diminishes body and mind... but not spirit.

Very gradually, over the years, all the systems of my body lose their effectiveness in keeping my body, including my brain, optimally healthy. If Guillain-Barre Syndrome had attacked me earlier in life, I would have undoubtedly regained strength, stamina and movement much faster. I'm three years beyond my diagnosis and I'm still working hard each day to bounce back.

The natural regenerating mechanisms of my body, the ones that rejuvenate me, have simply diminished in effectiveness over time. As I've aged, I have simply become less and less resilient to toxins, infections, imbalances and bodily attacks of all kinds.

I know very well that healthy aging doesn't happen on its own. Age alone does not automatically confer competence in "performing" this process we call aging well. Aging requires work; and this work needs to be quite intentional. So, I ask myself, *"What are the competencies of aging well?* I address this topic in my book titled "Even Better After 50" (available on Amazon at amzn.to/3a2LiAq).

This question gives the motive "push" to look at my own aging differently. If aging does have purpose, and I believe it does, then I, as a practitioner of aging, can address and embrace the process of aging with varying degrees of competence, and "perform" the overarching act of aging well... or not. I've seen many persons who could be "flunking" aging. I don't want to flunk aging.

There are building blocks to my health on all three levels.

One: Optimal physical health requires that I engage in: nutritious diet, generous exercise, no tobacco or other toxins, adequate sleep, moderate (or no) alcohol use, and the like.

Two: Optimal psychological and emotional health requires: stress reduction, stimulation of mind, healthy relationship connections, a positive outlook on life, clear thinking, being "in touch" with my feelings, making considered choices, and taking forthright action.

Three: Optimal soul or spiritual living requires addressing the spiritual developmental tasks appropriate for each stage and phase of life.

My research, concentrated observation of the human condition, and long hours studying, listening to and interacting with literally thousands of counseling patients has informed me to identify the physical, mental, and spiritual building blocks, or "tasks" that lead to optimal health in what I call the illumination years, ages 66 and beyond. Actually, I believe that there are sub-stages to the overall phase of life I call the "illumination years," that generally conform to the decades of our life. (1)

I certainly want to discover and practice the optimal living truths that form the foundation and the framework upon which I can build a solid life where I can radiate a glow of vitality, maximize my inherent gifts and strengths, optimize my physical and mental capacities, find purpose in life, and experience that internal sense of fulfillment we call "meaning."

The path of life, including aging, is my walk of a circle of life, a labyrinth-like journey of discovery that swings around and around again and again. As it does, I sometimes feel that I have walked this way before, yet even though the current part of the path seems so familiar to places I have walked before, it is actually a new and different part with a unique feel and special purpose all its own. As one task of optimal living wanes in importance, another task is simultaneously waxing.

I feel confident that I have dealt with, to a greater or lesser degree, the necessary developmental life tasks for growth up to this point. In former years, I have certainly felt the sting of physical change, I have developed increased self-awareness, I have taught and guided others, and to be sure I have become involved in many communities outside myself.

Yet, it is in my aging years when I spiral around to these tasks again, as it were, and deal with them in identifiably different ways than in the past. These tasks present themselves uniquely; the emphasis, intensity, comprehensiveness, and penetration of their place in later life energize them in ways that exert new and profound impact upon me. It's this profundity of presentation that gives these tasks their novelty and makes them stand-out in relief from other tasks in my aging years.

Each one of these tasks of aging is a soul journey unto itself. Each one is a trek that brings me closer to my real self, to my soul. I can choose to take-on the challenge, or I can choose to avoid, deny, or otherwise ignore the task altogether. When and if I do ignore them, I am choosing to abdicate my soul growth, I am barricading myself into a box of my own making that inhibits me and causes regressive and repressive repercussions in my life. Pain and spiritual fragmentation of one sort or another always find their way to my door when I refuse to take-on the challenges of my life.

I can think of the life changes that transitions bring either as opportunities that can enrich my life, or as threats to be avoided. The purpose of my search for enriched life meaning in my mature years is like a spirit-renewal the likes of which I have never seen in my life to date. When the responsibilities of one stage of life are lifted, a new forum for happiness emerges. This forum for change and growth is inside of me; it is the realm of my soul.

Part of the personal work necessary in my aging years is bringing my interior world into sharper focus, finding a more comfortable balance between my outside and my inside world. My continued growth and emerging happiness flows from my quest to discover new purpose, new meaning, and new life in my aging years.

My quest for my Authentic Self as I mature requires a clear head.

My path to happiness, fulfillment and life meaning is a continuous human unfolding of my authentic self … an ongoing expression of the full measure of my unique spiritual potential. I am endowed, as is each of us, with a cluster of 'spiritual DNA' that defines my spiritual potential and individualizes me/each of us from all other human beings on the earth.

Just as my material DNA is unique, and is the biological code which determines all of my physical attributes, i.e., eye and hair color, size, form, structure, strength, skin tone, shape, texture, etc., etc., etc., as well as my vulnerability to diseases, my immune system potency, and my physical mannerisms, to name but a few, so too, my spiritual DNA, if you will, determines an even broader array of spiritual potentials in me.

This so-called, spiritual DNA provides the raw material as well as the direction of my spiritual authenticity. Exactly the mechanism that determines my spiritual potential and the code that sets out the progression of my development, I don't know. What I do know is that my spiritual development requires my active and continuous participation.

There is never a time in my life, there is no stage where or when I can ever stop my volitional involvement in my ongoing spiritual growth. Just as I need to eat each and every day to ensure my physical survival, my onward physical growth and development, likewise I must take active steps every day to ensure my ongoing spiritual growth and development.

I need to perform work: body work, mind work, and spiritual work so I can better survive and even thrive. I call this work my 'tasks;' in the case of spiritual work, these are spiritual tasks. This work stimulates my onward, forward body, mind, and spirit development.

Aging is another reason why I imagine my morning Glory Day Brain Booster, my well formulated mix of God-given healing plants, forging their way through all the systems of my body regenerating what normal again has disturbed. I know I can't beat the aging process; I can't beat mortality but I want to do all I can to maximize every year of my life. I know I will die but until then I want to live as fully as I can every day. That's why I decided to start Glory Day.

Oxidation caused by free radicals in the environment can speed up the normal aspects of the aging process (2,3,4). Anti-oxidant supplements can inhibit the effects of free radicals in your system, helping you look and feel younger (5,6,7). All nine of the Glory Day Brain Booster ingredients are potent anti-oxidants, help to minimize the effects of aging and the damaging impact of these free radicals.

The benefits of each ingredient in addressing atherosclerosis, cardiovascular disease, diabetes, hypertension and brain pathology are also helpful in reducing damaging aspects of aging. And seven of the nine Glory Day ingredients have particular anti-aging benefits backed by scientific data:

1. Resveratrol: Resveratrol has been shown to activate longevity genes, modulate the hallmarks of aging including oxidative damage, inflammation, telomere attrition and cell senescence. It is believed to have positive effects on lifespan, age-related diseases and health maintenance. Resveratrol may help attenuate age-associated disorders by modulating age-related mechanisms. Resveratrol is the best-known substance for extending the lifespan of various organisms. It has gained widespread attention based on studies of its ability to extend the lifespan of yeast, worms, and flies, and its ability to protect against age-related diseases such as cancer, Alzheimer's, and diabetes in mammals. In one study, resveratrol extended fruit fly longevity by 41%! It also improved age-related symptoms such as locomotive deterioration, body weight gain, eye degeneration and neurodegeneration. It has shown benefits in mitochondrial metabolism and autophagy, which play a crucial role in regulating organism longevity. It appears to have a unique ability to extend the healthy years, or health span, of mammals and has potential to counteract the symptoms of age-related disease. Resveratrol is currently in preclinical tests in the Interventions Testing Program of the National Institute on Aging (8,9,10,11,12,13,14,15,16,17,19,34)

2. Curcumin: Curcumin has been shown to increase longevity and stress resistance in yeasts, nematodes, flies and mice. It also alleviated aging symptoms and postponed the progression of age-related diseases in which cellular senescence was involved. It eliminated

senescent cells, which has been shown to significantly improve the quality of life of mice. Curcumin reversed the mortality increase from heavy metal and environmental toxins in model systems. Curcumin is currently in preclinical tests in the Interventions Testing Program of the National Institute on Aging. Curcumin is a potent anti-inflammatory agent; shown to act by slowing the aging process and age-related diseases. (12,18,19,20,21,22,23)

3. Tamarisk and its ingredient Quercetin: Studies of Quercetin show it decreased senescent cells, alleviated physical dysfunction and increased survival by 36% while reducing mortality hazard to 65% in mice. Quercetin has shown neuroprotective effects, and reduced the impact of neurotoxic chemicals in models on neuronal injury and neurodegenerative diseases. It may stimulate cellular defenses against oxidative stress, induce autophagy, induce anti-oxidant and anti-inflammatory enzymes, restore plasma membrane damage, and have direct antioxidant effects. It prolonged lifespan in a yeast model. Quercetin is currently in preclinical tests in the Interventions Testing Program of the National Institute on Aging (12,17,19,24,25,26,27,28,34)

4. Bacopa: Bacopa has published effects of promoting neuron survival, acting as an anti-oxidant, and reducing structural and functional changes associated with aging. Bacopa is included in the Australian Research Council Longevity Intervention (ARCLI) study protocol looking at telomere length, cognitive,

biochemical and health measures in the elderly. (29,30,31,32)

5. Pine bark: Pine bark is a potent anti-oxidant, that has been shown to help maintain normal cellular function, reduce oxidative reaction and cell death. In mice studies of pine bark combined with other supplements, pine bark significantly increased lifespan and markedly reduced histopathology in the hippocampus, and reduced DNA fragmentation. It increased gene expression and helped protect cells from damage. Pine bark is included in the Australian Research Council Longevity Intervention (ARCLI) study protocol looking at telomere length, cognitive, biochemical and health measures in the elderly. (29,32,33)

6. DHA: DHA is a potential longevity promoter through mood and stress modulation. In combination with EPA, DHA increased median lifespan 15%, increased mitochondrial coupling, delayed lipid peroxidation, delayed onset of senescence, and aided mitochondrial metabolism in flies. It improved memory and longevity in mice. DHA has been shown to support brain cell survival and inhibit neuron cell death (34,35,36)

7. L-theanine: L-theanine demonstrated increased survival of roundworms. It is believed to protect nerves and has anti-oxidant and inti-inflammatory effects (37,38)

Chapter Eight

Reason 8: To Energize my Positive Mental Attitude and Overall Well-being

I was tired and feeling like I had lost my ever-present positive mental attitude, a bundle of life energy that I had come to take for granted. I felt weary and worn-down, mentally flabby and emotionally flat. After more than three years recuperating from Guillain-Barre: in-patient rehab for first six months, another six months of daily, all-day therapy, followed by outpatient therapy, my sense of inner well-being needed reactivation.

I was not fulfilling the two fundamental ingredients of "Positive Wellbeing" (PWB):

1) I didn't feel subjective happiness, and

2) I no longer felt that what I was doing with my life had a deep sense of meaning and purpose. (1)

My own clinical work counseling patients over the years had well-prepared me to see that I needed help. I fell fairly low on the PWB spectrum. Persons with PWB exhibit some, most, or even all of the behaviors on the Positive Wellbeing Scale. Before I started Glory Day Brain Booster, I scored 67. Where do you score?

Positive Wellbeing Scale

<u>Directions</u>: Rate each item on a 1 to 10 scale; 1 indicating the lowest agreement, and 10 the highest. Where do you fall in each of the items? Add your ten scores for a total, overall score.

1. I have evolved a generous view of others and of the world.

2. I am reflective and seek self-understanding.

3. I form a caring and positive relationship with nature.

4. I have the courage to change both myself and conditions around me.

5. I am sought out by others for counsel, wisdom, perspective and creative insight.

6. I am committed to continued learning.

7. I am clearly engaged in caring behaviors toward myself and others.

8. I have developed healthy eating and exercise patterns.

9. I find laughter and tears coming easily and spontaneously.

10. I am a hopeful person.

I felt I was starting to exhibit some of the characteristics of the people I talked about in one of the courses I teach: "How to Deal with 'Difficult' Personalities." I think my wife would confirm that I fulfilled some of the 'difficult' behaviors on the Difficult Personality Scale. Before I started Glory Day Brain Booster, I scored a 69. Where do you score?

Difficult Personality Scale

Directions: Rate each item on a 1 to 10 scale; 1 indicating the lowest agreement, and 10 the highest. Where do you fall in each of the items? Add your ten scores for a total, overall score.

1. A tendency to blame others for problems, and feelings of isolation.

2. Moodiness, irritability, thoughtlessness, low vitality.

3. Cling to rigid opinions, unable to set them aside long enough to listen to another's views or experiences.

4. A need to hang on to what was.

5. An increasing obsession with life's inequities and their wounds.

6. An excessive focus on themselves.

7. Fear of the future.

8. Feeling anxious, unsettled and dissatisfied… no peace.

9. Has assumed either an "in your face" attitude, or an "I don't care" attitude.

10. Little or no purpose in life. (2)

A recent study from the University of Nottingham, England uncovered 14 unique elements of well-being. (3)

- Happiness – feeling cheerful
- Vitality – feeling energetic
- Calmness – feeling relaxed
- Optimism – being hopeful
- Involvement – feeling engaged
- Awareness – being in-touch with feelings
- Acceptance – embracing yourself the way you are
- Self-worth – liking yourself
- Competence – feeling effective in what you do
- Development – feeling you are improving and advancing
- Purpose – having a life mission
- Significance – feeling worthwhile
- Congruence – feeling what you do and who you are overlap
- Connection – feeling close to people

I wanted to get out of the hole I fell into. I wanted to start looking up more, and down less. I wanted a fuller, richer, and more meaningful life. I wanted to feel the zest for living I formerly enjoyed. I needed someone to throw me a rope. That's when I found Glory Day Brain Booster.

Seven of the ingredients of Glory Day Brain Booster are backed-up by compelling research that they enhance overall mood and sense of wellbeing.

1. Curcumin: In human studies, curcumin reduced physical and mental fatigue, increased calmness, enhanced contentedness, improved sustained attention and improved resilience in response to stress. It appears to have an anti-fatigue effect. Numerous randomized controlled human clinical trials showed that curcumin reduced depression symptoms. (5,6,7)

2. Bacopa monnieri: Bacopa was shown to reduced anxiety and depression in randomized, double-blind, placebo-controlled trials (8,9,10)

3. Lion's Mane mushroom: The references included here showed evidence that lion's mane improves anxiety, fights fatigue, and data suggest a beneficial role in depression. (11,12,13)

4. Pine bark: Pine bark improves mood, fatigue, sleeping and sustained attention and reduces irritability in these studies (14,15,16,17)

5. L-Theanine: L-theanine studies demonstrated potential to relax the mind, increase attention and alertness, reduce stress and anxiety and improve sleep quality. L-theanine showed a statistically significant improvement in depression in an open label study (18,19,20,21,22,23,24,25)

6. Gingko biloba: In a human clinical study in elderly patients gingko biloba reduced depression and anxiety. (26)

7. Resveratrol: Anti-depressant effects of resveratrol were suggested in 22 animal studies. (27,28,29,30

My work over the years has all centered on inspiring healthy living in body, mind and spirit. Indeed, my counseling practice is called The Body, Mind & Spirit Center. When I survey my life's work, I see that it can be condensed into 12 competencies that together offer us the best "formula" for living a life well of body, wise of mind, and whole of spirit.

I'd like to send you my "Well, Wise & Whole" Questionnaire (short form) that you can take and score on your own, which gives you a score on each of these 12 mega-competencies, together with comparative scores from others who have taken the questionnaire.

E-mail me to receive your free personal wellness assessment:

drjohnson@lifelongadultministry.org

Chapter 9

Reason 9: To Smile More Freely and Frequently

I wasn't smiling like I used to... like I wanted to. I'm a big proponent of smiling as a way to activate positive feelings. I even wrote a book on the topic titled "The Power of Smiling" (available on Amazon at amzn.to/2JXunoe). I regularly give a copy to my counseling patients. Here is a glimpse of what's in the book...

Of all the tools in positive psychology's toolbox, smiling is perhaps the easiest to perform, the quickest acting, and the most effective in bringing about the tremendously positive effects discovered by positive psychology research.

Psychological research that looks at the effects of smiling all seems to arrive at a universal conclusion: smiling is the key to a positive outlook on life. The positive effects of smiling are legion: improved immune function, increased tolerance for pain and frustration, lowered stress and blood pressure, and even higher levels of creativity. (1)

Interestingly, and very importantly, the positive effects of smiling are seen whether the smile is

*genuine or "forced." Evidently the mind doesn't
know the difference and reacts similarly to either.*

Research also points to the fact that smiling has dramatic effects on personal interactions. Smiling seems to increase altruism; smiling people simply get more help/aid/assistance from others. Smiling people are more attractive and approachable than they otherwise would be.

Dr. Mark Stibich, Ph.D. offers us ten general ways that smiling affects us positively: relationally, emotionally, behaviorally, and psychologically. (2)

1. Smiling makes us attractive. We are drawn to people who smile. Frowns, scowls, and grimaces all push people away, but a smile draws them in.

2. Smiling changes our mood. It's hard to be "moody" when we're wearing a smile. A smile can "trick" our bodies into shifting our mood in a positive direction.

3. Smiling is contagious. A smile brightens up all those around us; it makes our lives happier.

4. Smiling relieves stress. Smiling saves us from appearing tired, worn down, and overwhelmed – all of which increase our internal stress levels.

5. Smiling boosts our immune system. Our immune system is hyper-sensitive to our mood; when we smile, we boost our mood which also strengthens our immune system making us less vulnerable to everything from colds and flu to infections of all types.

6. Smiling lowers our blood pressure. When we reduce our stress, we experience a corresponding decrease in hypertension (high blood pressure).

7. Smiling releases endorphins, natural painkillers, and serotonin. All of these are chemicals that our bodies naturally produce. Endorphins increase our overall sense of well-being. Natural painkillers fight pain of all types, and serotonin regulates our mood.

8. Smiling injects more tone, freshness, and vibrancy into our appearance. Smiling shapes our faces in such a way that we look younger. Smiling works like a natural face lift. Smiling is an anti-gravity "miracle drug" that re-sculpts our facial muscles and gives us a new vitality.

9. Smiling makes us seem more successful. Smiling raises our confidence level, gives us enhanced self-esteem, and improves our overall poise. All of these together give us an aura of success.

10. Smiling helps us stay positive. Smiling is our best "attitude adjustment." It's hard to think of something negative when we're smiling.

I knew, and I taught, that smiling does seem to bring about personality changes in a positive direction. The change potential of a smile can be experienced either internally or externally.

Internally, smiling offers much. When I smile...

- I generate a new mental attitude.
- I bring about a positive change in my insight and outlook.
- I shift my thoughts from negative to positive.
- I stimulate new, more positive emotional reactions.
- I activate new choices that bring personality growth.
- I am moved into action.

External changes are those that other people can see. While my attitudes, perceptions, thoughts, feelings, and even my decisions lay hidden beneath the surface, others do see my behaviors and actions... what I do! So, smiling has the power to actually change my behavior! This change is most important because it's only by my actions (behavior) that others come to see me, engage with me, and evaluate me. Fortunately or not, I am, and we all are, judged by our actions.

Start Smiling Again

I wanted to start smiling again. My personality was drooping; it certainly wasn't operating well enough to energize me, especially as I was trying to reclaim myself after three years of solid therapy. I needed a personality "perk-up"; I needed a personality tonic that would assist me to do what I knew I needed to do. I just couldn't seem to collect the necessary spark to ignite my "smiling mechanism". That's when I discovered Glory Day Brian Booster. The prospect of taking Glory Day gave me hope, and put a smile on my face.

Chapter Ten

Reason 10: To Develop New Resilience

Resilience is the capacity to heal, and grow yet stronger. How I prayed each day during my recuperative time (and still do) that all the hard therapeutic work would somehow bring healing. I wanted to drink deeply from the well of healing energy; I wanted to quench my thirst for change, for growth, for the energy that I needed for a resurgence of body, mind and Spirit. I wanted what I wrote about in my book titled, "Body, Mind, Spirit: Tapping the Healing Power Within" (available on Amazon at amzn.to/2VnTqG7).

I didn't necessarily pray for a cure; rather I prayed for healing. I knew that the medical/therapeutic community was doing all they could to bring me to a maximum performance level. They always asked me my goals for therapy. My standard response was that I wanted to walk and I wanted to keyboard again.

Here I am today able to walk with a cane and I am keyboarding as I write, but using only one finger that's in a brace. But I need healing: to shift my attitude about capabilities lost, efficiencies evaporated, and competencies compromised, so I can begin living fully once again. What I need is the great gift of resilience.

Resilience is the process of adapting well in the face of adversity, trauma, tragedy and/or threats. What power do I need to embrace this "process of adaptability"? I need the grace/power of resilience to know that I can change. I need a new expectation that I will change, and grow stronger in the process.

Perhaps my physical strength will never regain its former performance, but I need my inner strength and a renewed inner resolve to accept, not in submission or resignation, whatever improved level of capacity may emerge from all my work. If I can't be revived by resilience, I fear that I will slide into stagnation and immobility. I fear I will sink into a rigidity of heart and soul that will not only sour me, but emotionally cripple me. I fear that I might carry the burden of scowling at myself, at the people I love, and at the world that let me down. I might even become so spiritually contorted that I'd be tempted to "shake my fist" at my God who I would blame for somehow turning against me.

No, I need an intangible power to become my better self as a result of this new life journey. I need resilience.

Resilience is the capacity to recover from wounds, and rally from painful setbacks. I long to recover, to find not the old me, but a new me that, while physically not as able, is indeed a new me that can see new light in what otherwise is dismal darkness.

I certainly need to rally, but rally-power is not of the physical world. Rally-power comes from a precious intangible called courage, the grace/power I need to venture forth even in the face of the unknown, and in spite of my fear. Without courage I will simply languish into a tendency to avoid the difficult things I know I must face squarely. Yes, I need resilience.

Resilience is also the self-regulating tendency within me that can construct the "new normal" I need to recalibrate my life. To accomplish this goal I need new strength, the grace/power for constructive growth. I need strength to withstand the temptation of slipping back into a weakness of spirit, a deficiency of resolve; and ultimately giving up authentic living, only to retreat into mere existence.

I've seen, and I'm sure you have too, that some folks forfeit their lives to the unhealthy distractions the world offers us. Without the healing power of strength, I know I will backslide into a lifestyle dominated by never-ending TV, punctuated by adjusting my lounge chair, looking for my next meal, listening for the alarm signaling my next medication, and my outings to some corner of the medical community.

I didn't want this; I want to walk straight and tall with the power of healing activated within me. I need the capacity for sustained exertion. Without strength I will become rudderless and incapable, demoralized and perhaps even despondent. What a formula for depression!

Again, I need resilience! I need inner hardiness to change unfortunate situations into advantageous ones. I need to pull my brokenness away from the shadow of curse and put it under the light of blessing. I need the undergirding power that will allow my human spirit to prevail in spite of all the obstacles I may face.

I need all the components of resilience, including:

- Patience
- Perseverance
- Peace
- Faith
- Empathy
- Hope
- Wisdom
- Vision
- Humor

With this realization, and seeing that I had already started on a path to complacency, I discovered Glory Day Brain Booster. I read the research, some of which pointed to an opening of new energy, and promoting performance. It seemed to me that Glory Day Brain Booster might be worth a shot. I surveyed the research that supported my quest for the inner resolve of resilience.

1. Curcumin: Studies show curcumin promotes resilience to chronic social defeat stress, displaying a 4.5-fold increase in stress resilience as measured by social interaction test. Curcumin enhanced contentedness and increased norepinephrine levels (the feel-good neurotransmitter) (2,3,4,5)

2. Pine bark: Pine bark has been noted for improving mood, fatigue, sleeping and reducing irritability (5,6)

3. L-Theanine: It was observed that L-theanine relaxes the mind, increases alertness, and increases neurotransmitters (5,7,8,9,10)

4. Gingko biloba: Research evaluating gingko show it reduces anxiety and increases neurotransmitters (5,11)

5. Resveratrol: Resveratrol may induce brain resilience. (12,13,14)

References by Chapter

Chapter One

1. Amen, Daniel, G. MD, <u>Memory Rescue</u>, Tyndall – Momentum, Carol Stream, Illinois, 2013, page xix.
2. Parker, L. et al. Antioxidant activity and biologic properties of a procynaidin-rich extract from pine bark, pycnogenol. Review article. Free Radic Biol Med. 1999.
3. Pipingas A et al. Improved cognitive performance after dietary supplementation with a Pinus radiata bark extract formulation. Phytother Res. 2008 Sep
4. Belcaro G et al. Pycnogenol® improves cognitive function, attention, mental performance and specific professional skills in healthy professionals aged 35-55. J Neurosurg Sci. 2014 Dec
5. Belcaro G et al. The COFU3 Study. Improvement in cognitive function, attention, mental performance with Pycnogenol® in healthy subjects (55-70) with high oxidative stress. J Neurosurg Sci. 2015 Dec
6. Errichi S et al. Pycnogenol® supplementation improves cognitive function, attention and mental performance in students. Panminerva Med. 2011 Sep
7. Jai-Hong Cheng, et al. High molecular weight of polysaccharides from Hericium erinacens aganst amyloid beta-induced neurotoxicity. Complement Altern Med, 2016; 16:170. PMID 27266872.
8. Wilson S. Benefits of Lion's Mane Mushroom. Organic Daily Post 2018 Apr

9. Amori K at al. Improving effects of the mushroom Yamabushitake (Hericium erinaceus) on mild cognitive impairment: a double-blind placebo-controlled clinical trial. Phytother Res. 2009 Mar

10. Spelman K et al. Neurological Activity of Lion's Mane (Hericium erinaceus). Assoc for Advancement of Restorative medicine Dec 2017

11. Slough, L. et al. The chronic effects of an extract of Bacopa monnieri on cognitive function in healthy human subjects. Pschopharmocology, 2001.

12. Kongkeaw C et al. Meta-analysis of randomized controlled trials on cognitive effects of Bacopa monnieri extract. J Ethnopharmacology Jan 2014

13. Vollala V et al. Effect of Bacopa monniera Linn. (brahmi) extract on learning and memory in rats: A behavioral study. J Vet Behavior: Clinical Applications and Research 2010 Mar-Apr

14. Le X et al. Protective effects of Bacopa monnieri on ischemia-induced cognitive deficits in mice: The possible contribution of bacopaside I and underlying mechanism. J Ethnopharmacology Apr 2015

15. Uabundit N et al. Cognitive enhancement and neuroprotective effects of Bacopa monnieri in Alzheimer's disease model J Ethnopharmacology Jan 2010

16. Charles P et al. Bacopa monniera leaf extract up-regulates tryptophan hydroxylase (TPH2) and serotonin transporter (SERT) expression: Implications in memory formation. J Ethnopharmacology Mar 2011

17. Stough C et al. Examining the cognitive effects of a special extract of Bacopa Monniera (CDRI 08:KeenMind): A Review of 10 years of Research at Swinburne University. Journal of Pharmacy and Pharmaceutical Sciences Jun 2013

18. Stough C et al. The chronic effects of an extract of Bacopa monniera (Brahmi) on cognitive function in healthy human subjects. Psychopharmacology (Berl). 2001 Aug

19. Giesbrecht, T. et al. The combination of L-theanine and caffeine improves cognitive performance and increases subjective alertness. Pages 283-90, public online 19 Jul 2013.

20. Mancini E et al. Green tea effects on cognition, mood and human brain function: A systematic review. Phytomedicine. 2017 Oct

21. Dietz C et al. Effect of Green Tea Phytochemicals on Mood and Cognition. Curr Pharm Des. 2017

22. Fox J et al. Assessing the effects of caffeine and theanine on the maintenance of vigilance during a sustained attention task. Neuropharmacology. 2012 Jun

23. Park SK et al. A combination of green tea extract and l-theanine improves memory and attention in subjects with mild cognitive impairment: a double-blind placebo-controlled study. J Med Food. 2011 Apr

24. Nobre AC et al. L-theanine, a natural constituent in tea, and its effect on mental state. Asia Pac J Clin Nutr. 2008

25. Hidese S et al. Effects of chronic l-theanine administration in patients with major depressive

disorder: an open-label study. Acta Neuropsychiatr. 2017 Apr

26. White DJ et al. Anti-Stress, Behavioural and Magnetoencephalography Effects of an l-Theanine-Based Nutrient Drink: A Randomised, Double-Blind, Placebo-Controlled, Crossover Trial. Nutrients. 2016 Jan

27. Dodd FL et al. A double-blind, placebo-controlled study evaluating the effects of caffeine and L-theanine both alone and in combination on cerebral blood flow, cognition and mood. Psychopharmacology (Berl). 2015

28. Cao W et al. Resveratrol Boosts Cognitive Function by Targeting SIRT1. Neurochem Res. 2018 Sep

29. Shi Z et al. Resveratrol Attenuates Cognitive Deficits of Traumatic Brain Injury by Activating p38 Signaling in the Brain. Med Sci Monit. 2018 Feb

30. Navarro-Cruz AR et al. Effect of Chronic Administration of Resveratrol on Cognitive Performance during Aging Process in Rats. Oxid Med Cell Longev. 2017

31. Thaung ZJJ et al. Does phytoestrogen supplementation improve cognition in humans? A systematic review. Ann N Y Acad Sci. 2017 Sep

32. Evans HM et al. Clinical Evaluation of Effects of Chronic Resveratrol Supplementation on Cerebrovascular Function, Cognition, Mood, Physical Function and General Well-Being in Postmenopausal Women-Rationale and Study Design. Nutrients. 2016 Mar

33. Kou X et al. Resveratrol as a Natural Autophagy Regulator for Prevention and Treatment of Alzheimer's Disease. Nutrients. 2017 Aug

34. Turner RS et al. A randomized, double-blind, placebo-controlled trial of resveratrol for Alzheimer disease. Neurology. 2015 Oct

35. Evans HM et al. Effects of Resveratrol on Cognitive Performance, Mood and Cerebrovascular Function in Post-Menopausal Women; A 14-Week Randomised Placebo-Controlled Intervention Trial. Nutrients. 2017 Jan

36. Lee J et al. Examining the impact of grape consumption on brain metabolism and cognitive function in patients with mild decline in cognition: A double-blinded placebo controlled pilot study. Exp Gerontol. 2017 Jan

37. Hebi M et al. Hypolipidemic activity of Tamarix articulata Vahl. in diabetic rats. J Integr Med. 2017 Nov

38. Benmerache A et al. Chemical composition, antioxidant and antibacterial activities of Tamarix balansae J. Gay aerial parts. Nat Prod Res. 2017 Dec

39. Bettaib J et al. Tamarix gallica phenolics protect IEC-6 cells against H2O2 induced stress by restricting oxidative injuries and MAPKs signaling pathways. Biomed Pharmacother. 2017 May

40. Hmidene B et al. Inhibitory Activities of Antioxidant Flavonoids from Tamarix gallica on Amyloid Aggregation Related to Alzheimer's and Type 2 Diabetes Diseases. Biol Pharm Bull. 2017

41. Hebi M et al.   Potent antihyperglycemic and hypoglycemic effect of Tamarix articulata Vahl. in normal and streptozotocin-induced diabetic rats. Biomed Pharmacother. 2017 Mar

42. Mahfoudhi A et al.   Evaluation of Antioxidant, Anticholinesterase, and Antidiabetic Potential of Dry Leaves and Stems in Tamarix aphylla Growing Wild in Tunisia. Chem Biodivers. 2016 Dec

43. Cederholm T et al.   Omega-3 Fatty Acids in the Prevention of Cognitive Decline in Humans. ASN EB 2013 SYMPOSIA

44. Schaefer EJ et al.   Plasma phosphatidylcholine docosahexaenoic acid content and risk of dementia and Alzheimer disease: the Framingham Heart Study. Arch Neurol. 2006 Nov

45. Yurko-Mauro K et al. Docosahexaenoic acid and adult memory: a systematic review and meta-analysis. PLoS One. 2015 Mar

46. Welser M et al. Docosahexaenoic Acid and Cognition throughout the Lifespan. Nutrients. 2016 Feb

47. Yurko-Mauro K et al.   Beneficial effects of docosahexaenoic acid on cognition in age-related cognitive decline. Alzheimer's Dement. 2010 Nov

48. Goozee KG et al. Examining the potential clinical value of curcumin in the prevention and diagnosis of Alzheimer's disease. Br J Nutr. 2016 Feb

49. Cox KH et al. Investigation of the effects of solid lipid curcumin on cognition and mood in a healthy older population. J Psychopharmacol. 2015 May

50. Banji OJ et al. Curcumin and hesperidin improve cognition by suppressing mitochondrial dysfunction

and apoptosis induced by D-galactose in rat brain. Food Chem Toxicol. 2014 Dec

51. Liu D et al. Effects of curcumin on learning and memory deficits, BDNF, and ERK protein expression in rats exposed to chronic unpredictable stress. Behav Brain Res. 2014 Sep

52. Zhang L et al. Curcumin Improves Amyloid β -Peptide (1-42) Induced Spatial Memory Deficits through BDNF-ERK Signaling Pathway. PLoS One. 2015 Jun

53. Higden J et al Cognitive decline and Alzheimer's disease by Oregon State. Linus Pauling Institute Feb 2016

54. ...Yang, G. et al . Gingko Biloba for mild cognitive impairment and Alzheimer's disease: A systematic review and meta-analysis of randomized controlled trials. Curr Top Med Chem, 2016: 16(5): 520-8.

55. Sun M et al. Efficacy and Safety of Ginkgo Biloba Pills for Coronary Heart Disease with Impaired Glucose Regulation: Study Protocol for a Series of N-of-1 Randomized, Double-Blind, Placebo-Controlled Trials. Evid Based Complement Alternat Med. 2018 Oct

56. Zeng GR et al. Effect of Ginkgo biloba extract-761 on motor functions in permanent middle cerebral artery occlusion rats. Phytomedicine. 2018 Sep

57. Savaskan E et al. Treatment effects of Ginkgo biloba extract EGb 761® on the spectrum of behavioral and psychological symptoms of dementia: meta-analysis of randomized controlled trials. Int Psychogeriatr. 2018 Mar

58. McKeage K et al. Ginkgo biloba extract EGb 761® in the symptomatic treatment of mild-to-moderate

dementia: a profile of its use. Drugs Ther Perspect. 2018

Chapter Two

1. Johnson, R. P., Caregiving from Your Spiritual Strengths, AGES Press, St. Louis, 2013.
2. Lai, P.L., et al. Neurotrophic properties of Lion's Mane medicinal mushroom, Hericium erinaceus. J Med Mushrooms, 2013.
3. Wilson S. Benefits of Lion's Mane Mushroom. Organic Daily Post 2018 Apr
4. Lai PL et al. Neurotrophic properties of the Lion's mane medicinal mushroom, Hericium erinaceus (Higher Basidiomycetes) from Malaysia. Int J Med Mushrooms. 2013
5. Spelman K et al. Neurological Activity of Lion's Mane (Hericium erinaceus). Assoc for Advancement of Restorative Medicine Dec 2017
6. Wong KH et al. Neuroregenerative Potential of Lion's Mane Mushroom, Hericium erinaceus (Bull.: Fr.) Pers. (Higher Basidiomycetes), in the Treatment of Peripheral Nerve Injury. International Journal of Medicinal Mushrooms 2012
7. Vollala, V.R., et al. Enhancement of basolateral amygdaloid neuronal dendrite arborization following Bacopa monnieri extract treatment in adult rats. Clinic (Sao Paulo), 2011.
8. Kongkeaw C et al. Meta-analysis of randomized controlled trials on cognitive effects of Bacopa monnieri extract. J Ethnopharmacology Jan 2014

9. Le X et al. Protective effects of Bacopa monnieri on ischemia-induced cognitive deficits in mice: The possible contribution of bacopaside I and underlying mechanism. J Ethnopharmacology Apr 2015

10. Uabundit N et al. Cognitive enhancement and neuroprotective effects of Bacopa monnieri in Alzheimer's disease model J Ethnopharmacology Jan 2010

11. Stough C et al. Examining the cognitive effects of a special extract of Bacopa Monniera (CDRI 08:KeenMind): A Review of 10 years of Research at Swinburne University. Journal of Pharmacy and Pharmaceutical Sciences Jun 2013

12. Limpeanchob N et al. Neuroprotective effect of Bacopa monnieri on beta-amyloid-induced cell death in primary cortical culture. J of Ethnopharmacology Oct 2008

13. Ksouri, R. et al. Antioxidant antimicrobial activities of the edible medicinal halophyte Tammarix gallica L. and related polyphenolic constitutents. Food Chem Toxicology, 2009.

14. Urfi MK et al. The Role of Tamarix gallica Leaves Extract in Liver Injury Induced by Rifampicin Plus Isoniazid in Sprague Dawley Rats. J Diet Suppl. 2018 Jan

15. Bettaib J et al. Tamarix gallica phenolics protect IEC-6 cells against H2O2 induced stress by restricting oxidative injuries and MAPKs signaling pathways. Biomed Pharmacother. 2017 May

16. Fotuki, M. et al. Fish consumption, long chain Omega-3 fatty acids and risk of cognitive decline or

Alzheimer's disease: a complex association. Nat Clin Pract Neural, 2009, March 5: 140-52.

17. Cederholm T et al. Omega-3 Fatty Acids in the Prevention of Cognitive Decline in Humans. ASN EB 2013 SYMPOSIA

18. Schaefer EJ et al. Plasma phosphatidylcholine docosahexaenoic acid content and risk of dementia and Alzheimer disease: the Framingham Heart Study. Arch Neurol. 2006 Nov

19. Welser M et al. Docosahexaenoic Acid and Cognition throughout the Lifespan. Nutrients. 2016 Feb

20. Yurko-Mauro K et al. Beneficial effects of docosahexaenoic acid on cognition in age-related cognitive decline. Alzheimers Dement. 2010 Nov

21. Phillips, H.S. et al. BDNF mRNA is decreased in the hippocampus of individuals wth Alzheimer's disease. Online article, 2004.

22. Goozee KG et al. Examining the potential clinical value of curcumin in the prevention and diagnosis of Alzheimer's disease. Br J Nutr. 2016 Feb

23. Cox KH et al. Investigation of the effects of solid lipid curcumin on cognition and mood in a healthy older population. J Psychopharmacol. 2015 May

24. Banji OJ et al. Curcumin and hesperidin improve cognition by suppressing mitochondrial dysfunction and apoptosis induced by D-galactose in rat brain. Food Chem Toxicol. 2014 Dec

25. Lopresti ALet al. Curcumin for neuropsychiatric disorders: a review of in vitro, animal and human studies. J Psychopharmacol. 2017 Mar

26. Yang, G. et al . Gingko Biloba for mild cognitive impairment and   Alzheimer's disease: A systematic review and meta-analysis of randomized controlled trials. Curr Top Med Chem, 2016: 16(5): 520-8.
27. Yang G et al.   Ginkgo Biloba for Mild Cognitive Impairment and Alzheimer's Disease: A Systematic Review and Meta-Analysis of Randomized Controlled Trials. Curr Top Med Chem. 2016
28. Dai CX et al.   Role of Ginkgo biloba extract as an adjunctive treatment of elderly patients with depression and on the expression of serum S100B. Medicine (Baltimore). 2018 Sep
29. Zeng GR et al.   Effect of Ginkgo biloba extract-761 on motor functions in permanent middle cerebral artery occlusion rats. Phytomedicine. 2018 Sep
30. Granzotto, A. et al. Resveratrol and Alzheimer's disease: message in a bottle on red wine and cognition. Front Aging Neurosci, 2014, 6:96. PMID: 24860502.
31. Cao W et al.   Resveratrol Boosts Cognitive Function by Targeting SIRT1. Neurochem Res. 2018 Sep
32. Shi Z et al.   Resveratrol Attenuates Cognitive Deficits of Traumatic Brain Injury by Activating p38 Signaling in the Brain. Med Sci Monit. 2018 Feb
33. Navarro-Cruz AR et al.   Effect of Chronic Administration of Resveratrol on Cognitive Performance during Aging Process in Rats. Oxid Med Cell Longev. 2017
34. Evans HM et al.   Clinical Evaluation of Effects of Chronic Resveratrol Supplementation on Cerebrovascular Function, Cognition, Mood, Physical

Function and General Well-Being in Postmenopausal Women-Rationale and Study Design. Nutrients. 2016 Mar

35. Kou X et al. Resveratrol as a Natural Autophagy Regulator for Prevention and Treatment of Alzheimer's Disease. Nutrients. 2017 Aug

36. Turner RS et al. A randomized, double-blind, placebo-controlled trial of resveratrol for Alzheimer disease. Neurology. 2015 Oct

37. Lee J et al. Examining the impact of grape consumption on brain metabolism and cognitive function in patients with mild decline in cognition: A double-blinded placebo controlled pilot study. Exp Gerontol. 2017 Jan

38. Nobre, A.C., et a. L-Theanine, a natural constituent in tea, and its effect on mental state. Asia Pacific Journal of Clinical Nutrition, 2008.

39. Jamwal S et l. L-theanine prevent quinolinic acid induced motor deficit and striatal neurotoxicity: Reduction in oxido-nitrosative stress and restoration of striatal neurotransmitters level. Eur J Pharmacol. 2017 Sep

40. Ben P et al. L-Theanine attenuates cadmium-induced neurotoxicity through the inhibition of oxidative damage and tau hyperphosphorylation. Neurotoxicology. 2016 Dec

41. Lyon MR et al. The effects of L-theanine (Suntheanine®) on objective sleep quality in boys with attention deficit hyperactivity disorder (ADHD): a randomized, double-blind, placebo-controlled clinical trial. Altern Med Rev. 2011 Dec

42. Cho HS et al.   Protective effect of the green tea component, L-theanine on environmental toxins-induced neuronal cell death.   Neurotoxicology. 2008 Jul
43. Hidese S et al.   Effects of chronic l-theanine administration in patients with major depressive disorder: an open-label study.   Acta Neuropsychiatr. 2017 Apr
44. Türközü D et al. L-theanine, unique amino acid of tea, and its metabolism, health effects, and safety.   Crit Rev Food Sci Nutr. 2017 May
45. Kim TI et al. l-Theanine, an amino acid in green tea, attenuates beta-amyloid-induced cognitive dysfunction and neurotoxicity: reduction in oxidative damage and inactivation of ERK/p38 kinase and NF-kappaB pathways. Free Radic Biol Med. 2009 Dec
46. Scheff SW et al. Cognitive assessment of pycnogenol therapy following traumatic brain injury.   Neurosci Lett. 2016 Nov

Chapter Three

1. Johnson, R.P., Healing and Depression: Finding peace in the midst of transition, turmoil and/or illness. AGES Press, St. Louis, 2013.
2. Cox K et al. Investigation of the effects of solid lipid curcumin on cognition and mood in a healthy older population. Journal of Psychopharmacology 2015
3. Higden J et al Cognitive decline and Alzheimer's disease by Oregon State. Linus Pauling Institute Feb 2016

4. Sanmukhani, J. et al. Efficacy and safety of curcumin in major depressive disorder: a randomized controlled trial. Phytother. Res., 2014 Apr

5. Bhattacharya, S.K., et al. Anxiolytic activity of a standardized extract of Bacopa monnieri. Phytomeducine, 1998

6. Calabrese C et al. Effects of a standardized Bacopa monnieri extract on cognitive performance, anxiety, and depression in the elderly: a randomized, double-blind, placebo-controlled trial. J Altern Complement Med. 2008 Jul

7. Gupta GL et al. Bacopa monnieri abrogates alcohol abstinence-induced anxiety-like behavior by regulating biochemical and Gabra1, Gabra4, Gabra5 gene expression of GABAA receptor signaling pathway in rats. Biomed Pharmacother. 2019 Mar

8. Chin, C.H., et al. Erinacine A-Enriched Hericium erinaceus Mycelium produces anti-depressant-like effects. International Society of Molecular Science, 2018

9. Wilson S. Benefits of Lion's Mane Mushroom. Organic Daily Post 2018 Apr

10. Spelman K et al. Neurological Activity of Lion's Mane (Hericium erinaceus). Assoc for Advancement of Restorative Medicine Dec 2017

11. Belcaro G et al. Pycnogenol® improves cognitive function, attention, mental performance and specific professional skills in healthy professionals aged 35-55. J Neurosurg Sci. 2014 Dec

12. Belcaro G et al. The COFU3 Study. Improvement in cognitive function, attention, mental performance

with Pycnogenol® in healthy subjects (55-70) with high oxidative stress. J Neurosurg Sci. 2015 Dec

13. Errichi S et al. Pycnogenol® supplementation improves cognitive function, attention and mental performance in students. Panminerva Med. 2011 Sep

14. Errichi S et al. Supplementation with Pycnogenol® improves signs and symptoms of menopausal transition. Panminerva Med. 2011 Sep

15. Mancini E et al. Green tea effects on cognition, mood and human brain function: A systematic review. Phytomedicine. 2017 Oct

16. Dietz C et al. Effect of Green Tea Phytochemicals on Mood and Cognition. Curr Pharm Des. 2017

17. Fox J et al. Assessing the effects of caffeine and theanine on the maintenance of vigilance during a sustained attention task. Neuropharmacology. 2012 Jun

18. Park SK et al. A combination of green tea extract and l-theanine improves memory and attention in subjects with mild cognitive impairment: a double-blind placebo-controlled study. J Med Food. 2011 Apr

19. Nobre AC et al. L-theanine, a natural constituent in tea, and its effect on mental state. Asia Pac J Clin Nutr. 2008

20. White DJ et al. Anti-Stress, Behavioural and Magnetoencephalography Effects of an l-Theanine-Based Nutrient Drink: A Randomised, Double-Blind, Placebo-Controlled, Crossover Trial. Nutrients. 2016 Jan

21. Dodd FL et al. A double-blind, placebo-controlled study evaluating the effects of caffeine and L-theanine

both alone and in combination on cerebral blood flow, cognition and mood. Psychopharmacology (Berl). 2015

22. Hidese S et al. Effects of chronic l-theanine administration in patients with major depressive disorder: an open-label study. Acta Neuropsychiatr. 2017 Apr

23. Dai CX et al. Role of Ginkgo biloba extract as an adjunctive treatment of elderly patients with depression and on the expression of serum S100B. Medicine (Baltimore). 2018 Sep

24. Moore A et al. Resveratrol and Depression in Animal Models: A Systematic Review of the Biological Mechanisms. Molecules. 2018 Sep

25. Finnell JE et al. The protective effects of resveratrol on social stress-induced cytokine release and depressive-like behavior. Brain Behav Immun.2018 Jan

26. Hurley LL et al. Antidepressant Effects of Resveratrol in an Animal Model of Depression. Brain Behav Immun.2015 Jul

27. Liu L et al. Resveratrol counteracts lipopolysaccharide-induced depressive-like behaviors via enhanced hippocampal neurogenesis. Oncotarget. 2016 Aug

Chapter Four

1. Johnson, R.P., Healing Wisdom, AGES Press, St. Louis, 2012.
2. Wolters FJ et al. Coronary heart disease, heart failure, and the risk of dementia: A systematic review and meta-analysis. Alzheimers Dement. 2018 Nov;14(11)
3. Deckers K et al. Coronary heart disease and risk for cognitive impairment or dementia: Systematic review and meta-analysis. PLoS One. 2017 Sep 8;12(9)
4. Norton S et al. Potential for primary prevention of Alzheimer's disease: an analysis of population-based data. Lancet Neurol. 2014;13(8): 788–94
5. Kivimäki M et al. Physical inactivity, cardiometabolic disease, and risk of dementia: an individual-participant meta-analysis. BMJ. 2019 Apr 17;365
6. Verny M et al. Cognitive deficit, and neuropathological correlates, in the oldest-old. Rev Neurol (Paris). 2020 Mar 13
7. Kresge HA et al. Lower Left Ventricular Ejection Fraction Relates to Cerebrospinal Fluid Biomarker Evidence of Neurodegeneration in Older Adults. J Alzheimers Dis. 2020 Mar 2
8. Horrocks LA et al. Health benefits of docosahexaenoic acid (DHA). Pharmacol Res. 1999 Sep
9. Welser M et al. Docosahexaenoic Acid and Cognition throughout the Lifespan. Nutrients. 2016 Feb
10. Ghasemi F et al. How does high DHA fish oil affect health? A systematic review of evidence. Crit Rev Food Sci Nutr. 2019
11. Doughman SD et al. Omega-3 fatty acids for nutrition and medicine: considering microalgae oil as a

vegetarian source of EPA and DHA. Curr Diabetes Rev. 2007 Aug;3(3):198-203.

12. Kris-Etherton PM et al. Recent Clinical Trials Shed New Light on the Cardiovascular Benefits of Omega-3 Fatty Acids. Methodist Debakey Cardiovasc J. 2019 Jul-Sep;15(3):171-178

13. Dyck GJB et al. The Effects of Resveratrol in Patients with Cardiovascular Disease and Heart Failure: A Narrative Review. Int J Mol Sci. 2019 Feb

14. Sung MM et al. Resveratrol improves exercise performance and skeletal muscle oxidative capacity in heart failure. Am J Physiol Heart Circ Physiol. 2017 Apr

15. Matsumura N et al. Resveratrol improves cardiac function and exercise performance in MI-induced heart failure through the inhibition of cardiotoxic HETE metabolites. J Mol Cell Cardiol. 2018 Dec

16. Sun ZM et I. Resveratrol protects against CIH-induced myocardial injury by targeting Nrf2 and blocking NLRP3 inflammasome activation. Life Sci. 2020 Jan 27;245:117362

17. Sun M et al. Efficacy and Safety of Ginkgo Biloba Pills for Coronary Heart Disease with Impaired Glucose Regulation: Study Protocol for a Series of N-of-1 Randomized, Double-Blind, Placebo-Controlled Trials. Evid Based Complement Alternat Med. 2018 Oct

18. Ong LTD et al. Ginseng and Ginkgo Biloba Effects on Cognition as Modulated by Cardiovascular Reactivity: A Randomised Trial. PLoS One. 2016 Mar 3;11(3):e0150447

19. Tian J et al. Ginkgo Biloba Leaf Extract Attenuates Atherosclerosis in Streptozotocin-Induced Diabetic ApoE-/- Mice by Inhibiting Endoplasmic Reticulum Stress via Restoration of Autophagy through the mTOR Signaling Pathway. Oxid Med Cell Longev. 2019 Mar 18;2019:8134678

20. Wilson S. Benefits of Lion's Mane Mushroom. Organic Daily Post 2018 Apr

21. Spelman K et al. Neurological Activity of Lion's Mane (Hericium erinaceus). Assoc for Advancement of Restorative medicine Dec 2017

22. Yi Z et al. Protective Effect of Ethanol Extracts of Hericium erinaceus on Alloxan-Induced Diabetic Neuropathic Pain in Rats. Evidence-Based Complementary and Alternative Medicine 2015

23. Woi WS et al. Hypolipidaemic Effect of Hericium erinaceum Grown in Artemisia capillaris on Obese Rats. Mycobiology. 2013 Jun; 41(2): 94–99.

24. Cox KH et al. Investigation of the effects of solid lipid curcumin on cognition and mood in a healthy older population. J Psychopharmacol. 2015 May

25. 18. Kim TI et al. l-Theanine, an amino acid in green tea, attenuates beta-myloid-induced cognitive dysfunction and neurotoxicity: reduction in oxidative damage and inactivation of ERK/p38 kinase and NF-kappaB pathways. Free Radic Biol Med. 2009 Dec

Chapter Five

1. Johnson, R.P., From Cancer Survivor to New Life Thriver, AGES Press, St. Louis, 2019.
2. Johnson, R.P., The New Retirement: Discovering Your Dream, Retirement Options Press, St. Louis, 2001.
3. Wilken R et al. Curcumin: A review of anti-cancer properties and therapeutic activity in head and neck squamous cell carcinoma. Molecular Cancer 2011, 10:1
4. Devassy JG et al. Curcumin and cancer: barriers to obtaining a health claim. Nutr Rev. 2015 Mar;73(3):155-65
5. Wang Y et al. Curcumin in Treating Breast Cancer: A Review. J Lab Autom. 2016 Dec;21(6):723-731
6. Deguchi A et al. Curcumin targets in inflammation and cancer. Endocr Metab Immune Disord Drug Targets. 2015;15(2):88-96.
7. Rajamanickam V et al. Allylated Curcumin Analog CA6 Inhibits TrxR1 and Leads to ROS-Dependent Apoptotic Cell Death in Gastric Cancer Through Akt-FoxO3a. Cancer Manag Res. 2020 Jan 13;12:247-263
8. . Fathy Abd-Ellatef GE et al. Curcumin-Loaded Solid Lipid Nanoparticles Bypass P-Glycoprotein Mediated Doxorubicin Resistance in Triple Negative Breast Cancer Cells. Pharmaceutics. 2020 Jan 24;12(2)
9. Hosseini S et al. The effect of nanomicelle curcumin, sorafenib, and combination of the two on the cyclin D1 gene expression of the hepatocellular carcinoma cell line (HUH7). Iran J Basic Med Sci. 2019 Oct;22(10)

10. Mukherjee S et al. Using Curcumin to Turn the Innate Immune System Against Cancer. Biochem Pharmacol. 2020 Jan 24:113824

11.. Smagurauskaite G et al. New Paradigms to Assess Consequences of Long-Term, Low-Dose Curcumin Exposure in Lung Cancer Cells. Molecules. 2020 Jan 16;25(2)

12.. Jiang Z et al. Resveratrol and cancer treatment: updates. Ann N Y Acad Sci. 2017 Sep;1403(1):59-69

13.. Yousef M t al. Effects of Resveratrol against Lung Cancer: In Vitro and In Vivo Studies. Nutrients 2017 Nov 10;9(11)

14.. Gianchecchi E et al. Insights on the Effects of Resveratrol and Some of Its Derivatives in Cancer and Autoimmunity: A Molecule with a Dual Activity. Antioxidants (Basel). 2020 Jan 22;9(2)

15.. Fabian CJ et al. Omega-3 fatty acids for breast cancer prevention and survivorship. Breast Cancer Res. 2015 May 4;17:62

16.: Wang J et al. FFAR1-and FFAR4-dependent activation of Hippo pathway mediates DHA-induced apoptosis of androgen-independent prostate cancer cells. Biochem Biophys Res Commun. 2018 Nov 30;506(3)

17. Lin R et al. Dihydroartemisinin (DHA) induces ferroptosis and causes cell cycle arrest in head and neck carcinoma cells. Cancer Lett. 2016 Oct 10;381(1)

18.: Carrasco R et al. Prevention of doxorubicin-induced Cardiotoxicity by pharmacological non-hypoxic myocardial preconditioning based on Docosahexaenoic Acid (DHA) and carvedilol direct antioxidant effects: study protocol for a pilot, randomized, double-blind, controlled trial (CarDHA trial). Trials. 2020 Feb 4;21(1)

19. Gionfriddo Get al. Modulating Tumor-Associated Macrophage Polarization by Synthetic and Natural PPARγ Ligands as a Potential Target in Breast Cancer. Cells. 2020 Jan 10;9(1)

20. : Brito AF et al. Quercetin in Cancer Treatment, Alone or in Combination with Conventional Therapeutics? Curr Med Chem. 2015;22(26)

21. Reyes-Farias M et al. The Anti-Cancer Effect of Quercetin: Molecular Implications in Cancer Metabolism. Int J Mol Sci. 2019 Jun 28;20(13)

22. : Men K, et al. Nanoparticle-delivered quercetin for cancer therapy. Anticancer Agents Med Chem. 2014;14(6)

Chapter Six

1. Kongkeaw C et al. Meta-analysis of randomized controlled trials on cognitive effects of Bacopa monnieri extract. J Ethnopharmacology Jan 2014

2. Le X et al. Protective effects of Bacopa monnieri on ischemia-induced cognitive deficits in mice: The possible contribution of bacopaside I and underlying mechanism. J Ethnopharmacology Apr 2015

3. Uabundit N et al. Cognitive enhancement and neuroprotective effects of Bacopa monnieri in Alzheimer's disease model J Ethnopharmacology Jan 2010

4. Stough C et al. Examining the cognitive effects of a special extract of Bacopa Monniera (CDRI 08:KeenMind): A Review of 10 years of Research at Swinburne University. Journal of Pharmacy and Pharmaceutical Sciences Jun 2013

5. Stough C et al. The chronic effects of an extract of Bacopa monniera (Brahmi) on cognitive function in healthy human subjects. Psychopharmacology (Berl). 2001 Aug

6. Limpeanchob N et al. Neuroprotective effect of Bacopa monnieri on beta-amyloid-induced cell death in primary cortical culture. J of Ethnopharmacology Oct 2008

7. Goozee KG et al. Examining the potential clinical value of curcumin in the prevention and diagnosis of Alzheimer's disease. Br J Nutr. 2016 Feb

8. Cox KH et al. Investigation of the effects of solid lipid curcumin on cognition and mood in a healthy older population. J Psychopharmacol. 2015 May

9. Banji OJ et al. Curcumin and hesperidin improve cognition by suppressing mitochondrial dysfunction and apoptosis induced by D-galactose in rat brain. Food Chem Toxicol. 2014 Dec

10. Liu D et al. Effects of curcumin on learning and memory deficits, BDNF, and ERK protein expression in rats exposed to chronic unpredictable stress. Behav Brain Res. 2014 Sep

11. Zhang L et al. Curcumin Improves Amyloid β-Peptide (1-42) Induced Spatial Memory Deficits through BDNF-ERK Signaling Pathway. PLoS One. 2015 Jun

12. Lauritzen L et al. DHA Effects in Brain Development and Function. Nutrients. 2016 Jan 4;8(1)

13. : Cardoso C et al. Dietary DHA and health: cognitive function ageing. Nutr Res Rev. 2016 Dec;29(2)

14. . Dyall SC et al. Long-chain omega-3 fatty acids and the brain: a review of the independent and shared effects of EPA, DPA and DHA. Front Aging Neurosci. 2015 Apr 21;7:52

15. Loehfelm A et al. Docosahexaenoic acid prevents palmitate-induced insulin-dependent impairments of neuronal health. FASEB J. 2020 Feb 6.

16. Yang H et al. Flavangenol regulates gene expression of HSPs, anti-apoptotic and anti-oxidative factors to protect primary chick brain cells exposed to high temperature. J Therm Biol. 2019 Apr;81:1-11

17. Paarmann K et al. French maritime pine bark treatment decelerates plaque development and improves spatial memory in Alzheimer's disease mice. Phytomedicine. 2019 Apr;57:39-48

18. . Eryilmaz A et al. Protective effect of Pycnogenol on cisplatin-induced ototoxicity in rats. Pharm Biol. 2016 Nov;54(11):2777-2781

19. : Gao B et al. Pycnogenol Protects Against Rotenone-Induced Neurotoxicity in PC12 Cells Through Regulating NF-κB-iNOS Signaling Pathway. DNA Cell Biol. 2015 Oct;34(10)

20. Clark SP et al. Pine oil effects on chemical and thermal injury in mice and cultured mouse dorsal root ganglion neurons. Phytother Res. 2014 Feb;28(2):252-60

21.. Khan MM et al.   Protection of MPTP-induced neuroinflammation and neurodegeneration by Pycnogenol. Neurochem Int. 2013 Mar;62(4):379-88

22.: Siler-Marsiglio KI et al.   Protective mechanisms of pycnogenol in ethanol-insulted cerebellar granule cells. J Neurobiol. 2004 Nov;61(2)

23. Wilson S.   Benefits of Lion's Mane Mushroom. Organic Daily Post 2018 Apr

24. Lai PL et al.   Neurotrophic properties of the Lion's mane medicinal mushroom, Hericium erinaceus (Higher Basidiomycetes) from Malaysia. Int J Med Mushrooms. 2013

25. Spelman K et al. Neurological Activity of Lion's Mane (Hericium erinaceus).   Assoc for Advancement of Restorative medicine Dec 2017

26. Wong KH et al.   Neuroregenerative Potential of Lion's Mane Mushroom, Hericium erinaceus (Bull.: Fr.) Pers. (Higher Basidiomycetes), in the Treatment of Peripheral Nerve Injury.   International Journal of Medicinal Mushrooms 2012

27.. Yoneda Y.   An L-Glutamine Transporter Isoform for Neurogenesis Facilitated by L-Theanine.   Neurochem Res. 2017 Oct;42(10):2686-2697

28. Guo WL et al.   I-Theanine and NEP1-40 promote nerve regeneration and functional recovery after brachial plexus root avulsion.   Biochem Biophys Res Commun. 2019 Jan 22;508(4)

29. Urfi MK et al.   The Role of Tamarix gallica Leaves Extract in Liver Injury Induced by Rifampicin Plus Isoniazid in Sprague Dawley Rats.   J Diet Suppl. 2018 Jan 2;15(1):24-33

30. Bettaib J et al. Tamarix gallica phenolics protect IEC-6 cells against H2O2 induced stress by restricting oxidative injuries and MAPKs signaling pathways. Biomed Pharmacother. 2017 May;89:490-498

31. Costa LG et al. Mechanisms of Neuroprotection by Quercetin: Counteracting Oxidative Stress and More. Oxid Med Cell Longev. 2016;2016:2986796

32. Godoy JA et al. Quercetin Exerts Differential Neuroprotective Effects Against H2O2 and Aβ Aggregates in Hippocampal Neurons: the Role of Mitochondria. Mol Neurobiol. 2017 Nov;54(9)

33. Li YL et al. Quercetin protects neuronal cells from oxidative stress and cognitive degradation induced by amyloid β-peptide treatment. Mol Med Rep. 2017 Aug;16(2):1573-1577

34. Qiu J et al. Isoquercitrin promotes peripheral nerve regeneration through inhibiting oxidative stress following sciatic crush injury in mice. Ann Transl Med. 2019 Nov;7(22):680

35. Cao W et al. Resveratrol Boosts Cognitive Function by Targeting SIRT1. Neurochem Res. 2018 Sep;43(9):1705-1713

36. Kou X et al. Resveratrol as a Natural Autophagy Regulator for Prevention and Treatment of Alzheimer's Disease. Nutrients. 2017 Sep; 9(9): 927

37. Turner RS et al. A randomized, double-blind, placebo-controlled trial of resveratrol for Alzheimer disease. Neurology. 2015 Oct 20; 85(16)

Chapter Seven

1. Johnson, R. P., Even Better After 50, AGES Press, St. Louis, 2010.
2. Höhn A at al. Happily (n)ever after: Aging in the context of oxidative stress, proteostasis loss and cellular senescence. Redox Biol. 2017 Apr;11:482-501
3. Cabello-Verrugio C et al. Oxidative Stress in Disease and Aging: Mechanisms and Therapies. Oxid Med Cell Longev. 2016;2016:8786564
4. Martínez de Toda I et al. The role of Hsp70 in oxi-inflamm-aging and its use as a potential biomarker of lifespan. Biogerontology. 2015 Dec;16(6):709-21
5. Katta Ret al. An Anti-Wrinkle Diet: Nutritional Strategies to Combat Oxidation, Inflammation and Glycation Skin Therapy Lett. 2020 Mar;25(2):3-7
6. Nguyen HP et al. Sugar Sag: Glycation and the Role of Diet in Aging Skin. Skin Therapy Lett. 2015 Nov;20(6):1-5
7. Draelos ZD. Aging skin: the role of diet: facts and controversies. Clin Dermatol. 2013 Nov-Dec;31(6):701-6.
8. Li YR et al. Effect of resveratrol and pterostilbene on aging and longevity. Biofactors. 2018 Jan;44(1):69-82
9. Islam MS et al. Effect of the Resveratrol Rice DJ526 on Longevity. Nutrients. 2019 Aug 5;11(8)
10. Bhullar KS et al. Lifespan and healthspan extension by resveratrol. Biochim Biophys Acta. 2015 Jun;1852(6):1209-18
11. Faragher RGA et al. Resveralogues: From Novel Ageing Mechanisms to New Therapies? Gerontology. 2020 Jan 8:1-7

12. Gabandé-Rodríguez E et al. Control of Inflammation by Calorie Restriction Mimetics: On the Crossroad of Autophagy and Mitochondria. Cells. 2019 Dec 28;9(1)
13. Russo GL et al. Mechanisms of aging and potential role of selected polyphenols in extending healthspan. Biochem Pharmacol. 2019 Nov 21:113719
14. Panchenko AV et al. Comparative analysis of experimental data about the effects of various polyphenols on lifespan and aging. Adv Gerontol. 2019;32(3):325-330
15. Cheng CK et al. Pharmacological basis and new insights of resveratrol action in the cardiovascular system. Br J Pharmacol. 2019 Jul 26
16. Costa D et al. Genetic background, epigenetic factors and dietary interventions which influence human longevity. Biogerontology. 2019 Oct;20(5):605-626
17. Gómez-Linton DR et al. Some naturally occurring compounds that increase longevity and stress resistance in model organisms of aging. Biogerontology. 2019 Oct;20(5):583-603.
18. Bielak-Zmijewska A et al. The Role of Curcumin in the Modulation of Ageing. Int J Mol Sci. 2019 Mar 12;20(5)
19. Zhao Y et al. The Beneficial Effects of Quercetin, Curcumin, and Resveratrol in Obesity. Oxid Med Cell Longev. 2017;2017:1459497
20. Sadowska-Bartosz I et al. Effect of antioxidants supplementation on aging and longevity. Biomed Res Int. 2014;2014:404680.

21. Abolaji AO et al. Curcumin attenuates copper-induced oxidative stress and neurotoxicity in Drosophila melanogaster. Toxicol Rep. 2020 Jan 27;7:261-268
22. Kim BK et al. Cur2004-8, a synthetic curcumin derivative, extends lifespan and modulates age-related physiological changes in Caenorhabditis elegans. Drug Discov Ther. 2019;13(4):198-206
23. Sikora, E. et al. Immunological Ageing, 2010.
24. Xu M et al. Senolytics improve physical function and increase lifespan in old age. Nat Med. 2018 Aug;24(8):1246-1256
25. Costa LG et al. Mechanisms of Neuroprotection by Quercetin: Counteracting Oxidative Stress and More. Oxid Med Cell Longev. 2016;2016:2986796
26. Sunthonkun P et al. Life-span extension by pigmented rice bran in the model yeast Saccharomyces cerevisiae. Sci Rep. 2019 Dec 2;9(1):18061
27. Justice JN et al. Senolytics in idiopathic pulmonary fibrosis: Results from a first-in-human, open-label, pilot study. EBioMedicine. 2019 Feb;40:554-563
28. Ogrodnik M et al. Obesity-Induced Cellular Senescence Drives Anxiety and Impairs Neurogenesis. Cell Metab. 2019 May 7;29(5):1061-1077.e8
29. Simpson T et al. The Australian Research Council Longevity Intervention (ARCLI) study protocol (ANZCTR12611000487910) addendum: neuroimaging and gut microbiota protocol. Nutr J. 2019 Jan 5;18(1):1
30. Phulara SC et al. Bacopa monnieri promotes longevity in Caenorhabditis elegans under stress conditions. Pharmacogn Mag. 2015 Apr-Jun;11(42):410-6

31. Singh HK et al. Brain enhancing ingredients from Āyurvedic medicine: quintessential example of Bacopa monniera, a narrative review. Nutrients. 2013 Feb 6;5(2):478-97

32. Stough CK et al. A randomized controlled trial investigating the effect of Pycnogenol and Bacopa CDRI08 herbal medicines on cognitive, cardiovascular, and biochemical functioning in cognitively healthy elderly people: the Australian Research Council Longevity Intervention (ARCLI) study protocol (ANZCTR12611000487910). Nutr J. 2012 Mar 6;11:11

33. Veurink G et al. Reduction of inclusion body pathology in ApoE-deficient mice fed a combination of antioxidants. Free Radic Biol Med. 2003 Apr 15;34(8):1070-7

34. Rangaraju S et al. Mood, stress and longevity: convergence on ANK3. Mol Psychiatry. 2016 Aug;21(8):1037-49

35. Champigny CM et al. Omega-3 Monoacylglyceride Effects on Longevity, Mitochondrial Metabolism and Oxidative Stress: Insights from Drosophila melanogaster. Mar Drugs. 2018 Nov 16;16(11)

36. Ueda Y et al. Effect of dietary lipids on longevity and memory in the SAMP8 mice. J Nutr Sci Vitaminol (Tokyo). 2011;57(1):36-41

37. Zarse K et al. L-Theanine extends lifespan of adult Caenorhabditis elegans. Eur J Nutr. 2012 Sep;51(6):765-8

38. Jamwal S et al. L-theanine prevent quinolinic acid induced motor deficit and striatal neurotoxicity: Reduction in oxido-nitrosative stress and restoration

of striatal neurotransmitters level. Eur J Pharmacol. 2017 Sep 15;811:171-179

Chapter Eight

1. "What is the Psychology of Wellbeing?" www.robertsoncooper.com, December 16, 2018.
2. Johnson, R. P., The 12 Keys to Spiritual Vitality. Liguori Press, Liguori, MO. 1999.
3. Johnson, R.P., unpublished. 2019.
4. Longo, Y., & Joseph, S. The Scales of general well-being. Personality and Individual Differences, 109, 148-158. 2017.
5. Cox K et al. Investigation of the effects of solid lipid curcumin on cognition and mood in a healthy older population. Journal of Psychopharmacology 2015
6. Higden J et al Cognitive decline and Alzheimer's disease by Oregon State. Linus Pauling Institute Feb 2016
7. Sanmukhani, J. et al. Efficacy and safety of curcumin in major depressive disorder: a randomized controlled trial. Phytother. Res., 2014 Apr
8. Bhattacharya, S.K., et al. Anxiolytic activity of a standardized extract of Bacopa monnieri. Phytomeducine, 1998
9. Calabrese C et al. Effects of a standardized Bacopa monnieri extract on cognitive performance, anxiety, and depression in the elderly: a randomized, double-blind, placebo-controlled trial. J Altern Complement Med. 2008 Jul
10. Gupta GL et al. Bacopa monnieri abrogates alcohol abstinence-induced anxiety-like behavior by

regulating biochemical and Gabra1, Gabra4, Gabra5 gene expression of GABAA receptor signaling pathway in rats. Biomed Pharmacother. 2019 Mar

11. Chin, C.H., et al. Erinacine A-Enriched Hericium erinaceus Mycelium produces anti-depressant-like effects. International Society of Molecular Science, 2018

12. Wilson S. Benefits of Lion's Mane Mushroom. Organic Daily Post 2018 Apr

13. Spelman K et al. Neurological Activity of Lion's Mane (Hericium erinaceus). Assoc for Advancement of Restorative Medicine Dec 2017

14. Belcaro G et al. Pycnogenol® improves cognitive function, attention, mental performance and specific professional skills in healthy professionals aged 35-55. J Neurosurg Sci. 2014 Dec

15. Belcaro G et al. The COFU3 Study. Improvement in cognitive function, attention, mental performance with Pycnogenol® in healthy subjects (55-70) with high oxidative stress. J Neurosurg Sci. 2015 Dec

16. Errichi S et al. Pycnogenol® supplementation improves cognitive function, attention and mental performance in students. Panminerva Med. 2011 Sep

17. Errichi S et al. Supplementation with Pycnogenol® improves signs and symptoms of menopausal transition. Panminerva Med. 2011 Sep

18. Mancini E et al. Green tea effects on cognition, mood and human brain function: A systematic review. Phytomedicine. 2017 Oct

19. Dietz C et al. Effect of Green Tea Phytochemicals on Mood and Cognition. Curr Pharm Des. 2017

20. Fox J et al. Assessing the effects of caffeine and theanine on the maintenance of vigilance during a sustained attention task. Neuropharmacology. 2012 Jun

21. Park SK et al. A combination of green tea extract and l-theanine improves memory and attention in subjects with mild cognitive impairment: a double-blind placebo-controlled study. J Med Food. 2011 Apr

22. Nobre AC et al. L-theanine, a natural constituent in tea, and its effect on mental state. Asia Pac J Clin Nutr. 2008

23. White DJ et al. Anti-Stress, Behavioural and Magnetoencephalography Effects of an l-Theanine-Based Nutrient Drink: A Randomised, Double-Blind, Placebo-Controlled, Crossover Trial. Nutrients. 2016 Jan

24. Dodd FL et al. A double-blind, placebo-controlled study evaluating the effects of caffeine and L-theanine both alone and in combination on cerebral blood flow, cognition and mood. Psychopharmacology (Berl). 2015

25. Hidese S et al. Effects of chronic l-theanine administration in patients with major depressive disorder: an open-label study. Acta Neuropsychiatr. 2017 Apr

26. Dai CX et al. Role of Ginkgo biloba extract as an adjunctive treatment of elderly patients with depression and on the expression of serum S100B. Medicine (Baltimore). 2018 Sep

27. Moore A et al. Resveratrol and Depression in Animal Models: A Systematic Review of the Biological Mechanisms. Molecules. 2018 Sep
28. Finnell JE et al. The protective effects of resveratrol on social stress-induced cytokine release and depressive-like behavior. Brain Behav Immun.2018 Jan
29. Hurley LL et al. Antidepressant Effects of Resveratrol in an Animal Model of Depression. Brain Behav Immun.2015 Jul
30. Liu L et al. Resveratrol counteracts lipopolysaccharide-induced depressive-like behaviors via enhanced hippocampal neurogenesis. Oncotarget. 2016 Aug

Chapter Nine

1. Johnson, R.P., The Power of Smiling, AGES Press, St. Louis, 2014.
2. Stibich,M. http://longevity.about.com/od/lifelongbeauty/tp/smiling.htm?p=1

Chapter Ten

1. Johnson, R.P., Freedom from Low Self-Esteem. AGES Press, St. Louis, 2019.
2. Aubry AV et al. A diet enriched with curcumin promotes resilience to chronic social defeat stress. Neuropsychopharmacology. 2019 Mar;44(4):733-742.
3. . Cox KH et al. Investigation of the effects of solid lipid curcumin on cognition and mood in a healthy older

population. J Psychopharmacol. 2015 May;29(5):642-51

4. Nishikawa S et al. Co-Administration of Curcumin and Artepillin C Induces Development of Brown-Like Adipocytes in Association with Local Norepinephrine Production by Alternatively Activated Macrophages in Mice. J Nutr Sci Vitaminol (Tokyo). 2019;65(4):328-334

5. Trebatická J et al. Psychiatric Disorders and Polyphenols: Can They Be Helpful in Therapy? Oxid Med Cell Longev. 2015;2015:248529

6. Belcaro G et al. Pycnogenol® improves cognitive function, attention, mental performance and specific professional skills in healthy professionals aged 35-55. J Neurosurg Sci. 2014 Dec

7. Mancini E et al. Green tea effects on cognition, mood and human brain function: A systematic review. Phytomedicine. 2017 Oct

8. Dietz C et al. Effect of Green Tea Phytochemicals on Mood and Cognition. Curr Pharm Des. 2017

9. Nobre AC et al. L-theanine, a natural constituent in tea, and its effect on mental state. Asia Pac J Clin Nutr. 2008

10. White DJ et al. Anti-Stress, Behavioural and Magnetoencephalography Effects of an l-Theanine-Based Nutrient Drink: A Randomised, Double-Blind, Placebo-Controlled, Crossover Trial. Nutrients. 2016 Jan

11. Dodd FL et al. A double-blind, placebo-controlled study evaluating the effects of caffeine and L-theanine both alone and in combination on cerebral blood flow,

cognition and mood. Psychopharmacology (Berl). 2015

12. Savage K et al. GABA-modulating phytomedicines for anxiety: A systematic review of preclinical and clinical evidence. Phytother Res. 2018 Jan;32(1):3-18

13. Finnell JE et al. The protective effects of resveratrol on social stress-induced cytokine release and depressive-like behavior. Brain Behav Immun.2018 Jan

14. Corpas R et al. Resveratrol Induces Brain Resilience Against Alzheimer Neurodegeneration Through Proteostasis Enhancement. Mol Neurobiol. 2019 Feb;56(2):1502-1516

Appendix One

Your Personality

Who or what runs your personality? This may seem a ridiculous question but I can assure you it's not.

The way you use your personality (yes, you are supposed to be the director of your personality) will determine how well you run your life and ultimately decide the vigor and hardiness of your overall wellness.

Your personality, and mine, operates by continuously performing six functions. As you perform these six functions well, and use them with intentionality, you will live a more positive life. Here are the six functions:

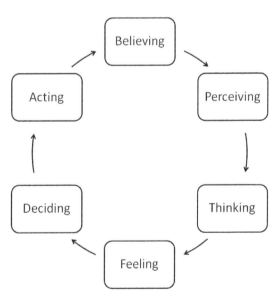

My book, titled "Discover Your Spiritual Strengths" (available on Amazon at amzn.to/3b3vzCv) thoroughly describes these six personality functions. You can find a description of the book on my website, www.spiritualstrengths.org.

I recommend this book if you'd like to take a "deeper dive" into understanding your personality better, and how to take clearer and stronger command of it.

For an even deeper personal dive, I can also recommend taking the Spiritual Strengths Profile (SSP), a 120 item spiritual personality questionnaire that generates a 20 page report that among other things identifies your strongest virtue in each of the six functions of your personality, and their corresponding shadow and compulsion. Find the SSP on the same website.

Appendix Two

The Spiritual Strengths Profile (SSP)

Each of your six personality functions is "powered" by a virtue (spiritual strength) that provides the energy to keep it going healthfully.

The SSP is a 120 item spiritual development inventory that identifies and thoroughly describes your six signature spiritual strengths (virtues) organized in framework of your six personality functions.

The SSP is the next generation of spiritual development inventories. It is several steps beyond the Enneagram and certainly beyond even the most popular personality inventory today.

Your individual "Spiritual Strengths Type" (your six signature spiritual strengths) gives you practical and personal information you can find nowhere else, and from which you can formulate a basic plan for spiritual strengths growth, development and inner healing. The SSP provides a forward looking, clear-eyed direction for positive self-change simply yet powerfully.

Beyond your six spiritual strengths, the SSP also identifies your personality healing blocks. Each of your spiritual strengths has a...

1) **Shadow**, a "place" where the power of the strength is in darkness, creating a spiritual blind spot. Each of your strengths also has a...

2) **Compulsion** which becomes activated when you, quite unknowingly, allow your ego (false self) to become over-active and start taking over your personality. Your SSP results pinpoint these spiritual blocks for you. Both shadows and compulsions create separation from your inner strengths.

Go to: www.spiritualstrengths.org where you can learn more about the SSP and take the SSP online.

Appendix Three

Books in the Spiritual Strengths Inner Healing Series

By Richard P. Johnson, PhD

1. God Give Me Strength! Finding the Inner Power Necessary to Turn Your Illness Around

2. Discover Your Spiritual Strengths: Find Health, Healing, and Happiness (flagship book of the Plan)

3. Body, Mind, Spirit: Tapping the Healing Power Within

4. Prayers for Healing... Physical Illnesses, Emotional Broken Places, an/or Spiritual Dis-eases

5. The Ten Most Effective Spiritual Self-Care Techniques for Healing

6. Smiling Through Whatever Life Brings: Using Positive Psychology for Healing

7. Healing Wisdom: 101 Spiritual Truths for Accelerating Healing

8. Healing and Depression: Finding Peace in the Midst of Transition, Turmoil, or Illness

9. Living from Your Spiritual Center: Constructing Your Personal Healing Program

10. Finding Your Significance: Constructing a Full Life Beyond Your Life-Trials

For Caregivers...

1. Caregiving from Your Spiritual Strengths: The Ten Fundamental Principles for Optimal Success

2. Because I Care... Inspiration for Caregiving for Spouses, Health Care Personnel, Family & Friends

Find descriptions of each of these books on...

www.spiritualstrengths.org

Appendix Four

Books in the Spiritual Strengths Cancer Series

By Richard P. Johnson, PhD

1. From Survivor to New Life Thriver: Living Your Best Life After Cancer

2. Discover Your Spiritual Strengths: Find Health, Healing, and Happiness

3. Cancer Healing Prayers for a New Tomorrow: Heal Your Body, Illuminate Your Mind, Awaken Your Spirit

4. Spiritual Self-Care - The Ten Most Effective Self-Care Techniques for Healing Your Cancer

5. Smiling Through Cancer: Using Positive Psychology to Tap Into God's Healing Power in Your Soul

6. Cancer Wisdom: 101 Spiritual Truths that Can Heal Your Cancer

7. Cancer and Depression: Finding Peace, Harmony, and Joy in the Midst of Turmoil

8. Maintaining Your Spiritual Center in the Midst of Cancer

9. Finding Your Significance after Cancer: Constructing Your Best Life

For Cancer Caregivers...

10. Because I Care: Spirit-Motivated Cancer Caregiving for Spouses, Healthcare Personnel, Family Members, and Friends

11. Cancer Care: The 10 Fundamental Caregiving Principles for Optimal Caregiving Success

Find descriptions of each of these books on...

www.spiritualstrengths.org

Appendix Five

Books on Positive Living & Vital Aging

1. Johnson, R. P., My Memory Is Awakening: My First 30 Days Taking Glory Day Brain Booster, AGES Press, St. Louis, 84 pages, 2020.

2. Johnson, R. P., Freedom from Low Self-Esteem, AGES Press, St. Louis, 160 pages, 2019.

3. Johnson, R. P., Even Better After 50: How to Become (and remain) Well of Body, Wise of Mind, and Whole of Spirit, AGES Press, St. Louis, 238 pages, 2010.

4. Johnson, R. P., ReCareer: Find Your Authentic Work in the Second Half of Life, AGES Press, St. Louis, 257 pages, 2009.

5. Johnson, R. P., Parish Ministry for Maturing Adults: Principles, Plans, and Bold Proposals, Twenty-Third Publications, New London, CT, 120 pages, 2007, revised 2019.

6. Johnson, R.P. The Nun and the Doctor: A Conversion/Love Story at Midlife, (novel) AGES Press, 278 pages, 2004.

7. Johnson, R.P. Loving for a Lifetime: Six Essentials for a Happy, Healthy, and Holy Marriage, Liguori Publications, 128 pages, 2002.

8. Johnson, R.P. The New Retirement: Discovering Your Dream, World Press, St. Louis, 121 pages, 2001.

9. Johnson, R.P. All My Days: Personal Life Review, Liguori Publications, 80 pages, 2000.

10. Johnson, R.P. Creating a Successful Retirement: Finding Peace and Purpose, Liguori Publications, 176 pages, 1999. (Catholic Press Assn. award winner)

11. Johnson, R.P. How to Honor Your Aging Parents: The Ten Fundamental Principles of Caregiving, Liguori Publications, 127 pages, 1999.

12. Johnson, R.P. 12 Keys of Spiritual Vitality: Powerful Lessons in Living Agelessly, Liguori Publishing, Liguori, MO, 176 pages, 1998. (Catholic Press Assn. award winner)

13. Johnson, R.P. Caring for Aging Parents, Concordia Publishing Co., St. Louis, 190 pages, 1995.

14. Johnson, R.P. A Christian's Guide to Mental Wellness: Balancing Between (Not Choosing Between) Psychology and Religion, Liguori Publishing, Liguori, MO, 160 pages, 1990.

15. Johnson, R.P. Aging Parents-How to Understand and Help Them, Liguori Publishing, Liguori, MO, 110 pages, 1987.

Find descriptions of each of these books on…

www.senioradultministry.com

Appendix Six

Brain Booster

Made in the USA
Las Vegas, NV
28 February 2021